A DANGEROUS JOB

PREVIOUS BOOKS BY DIANA HENDRY

Poetry

Making Blue, Peterloo Poets, 1995

Borderers, Peterloo Poets, 2001

Twelves Lilts: Psalms & Responses, Mariscat Press, 2003

Sparks! (with Tom Pow), Mariscat Press, 2005

Late Love & Other Whodunnits, Peterloo Poets/Mariscat
  Press, 2008

The Seed-box Lantern: New & Selected Poems, Mariscat
  Press, 2013

Second Wind (with Douglas Dunn and Vicki Feaver), The Saltire
  Society, 2015

The Watching Stair, Worple Press, 2018

Where I Was, Mariscat Press, 2020

The Guest Room, Worple Press, 2022

Fiction

My Father as an Ant, Postbox Press, 2017

Children's Books

Christmas in Exeter Street, (illus. John Lawrence), Julia MacRae/
  Walker books, 1989

Double Vision, Julia MacRae/Walker Books, 1990

The Very Noisy Night, (illus. Jane Chapman), 1990

Harvey Angell, Julia MacRae/Red Fox, 1991

The Seeing, Bodley Head/Corgi, 2012

Out of the Clouds, Hodder, 2016

Whoever You Are, Hodder, 2018

You Can't Cuddle a Crocodile, (illus. Ed Eaves), Hachette, 2019

A DANGEROUS JOB

& Other Essays

DIANA HENDRY

Printed by imprintdigital
Upton Pyne, Exeter
www.digital.imprint.co.uk

Typesetting and cover design by The Book Typesetters
hello@thebooktypesetters.com
07422 598 168
www.thebooktypesetters.com

Published by Shoestring Press
19 Devonshire Avenue, Beeston, Nottingham, NG9 1BS
(0115) 925 1827
www.shoestringpress.co.uk

First published 2024
© Copyright: Diana Hendry
© Cover image: 'The Lure of Books', an illustration from
   A Gallery of Girls by C. Coles Phillips

The moral right of the author has been asserted.

ISBN 978-1-915553-52-2

For Robyn Marsack – with love

CONTENTS

HALCYON DAYS

It begins when I get a job in the Literary Department of *The Sunday Times*. I call myself a secretary but actually I'm defined as a shorthand-typist. I'm slightly better at typing than at shorthand because I have pianist's fingers and can go prestissimo on any machine. My shorthand is more adagio but reasonable enough so that when I can't read back a word I can at least make up one that seems to fit.

I'm shorthand-typist/secretary to the Assistant Literary Editor, J.W. Lambert and I have never been happier. I'm happy without knowing it. I'm happy in the way you only recognise later when you're not happy.

I'm happy because I'm surrounded by books and because no-one minds me reading them and because for all of my 19 years I've been very short of books. Let me put that another way. Deprived of books. I'm the eight year old reading with a torch under the blankets. I'm the twelve year old given a bicycle to get her outside, away from books. I'm the fourteen year old enrolling the whole family in the library so I can use their tickets. And so on. God bless the grandfather who occasionally bought me one.

And then, in my first job in London – an American oil company, based in Piccadilly – I'm sacked for reading, even though I don't read when I should be typing, only when there isn't any typing to do. So I'm not quite sure how I've landed this job at *The Sunday Times* unless someone wrote me a reference saying my typing was good but they weren't happy with my reading and someone, maybe JWL or maybe even the Literary Editor himself, Leonard Russell, laughed and said 'we'll have her!'

At first, in the Literary Department, I'm still so jumpy about reading that I'm constantly poised to hide my book under the desk. Then Jack Lambert blows in, gives me a 'good morning' and clearly thinks it's the most natural thing in the world to find someone reading. And so does the assistant Assistant Literary

Editor, Michael Ratcliffe, who is not much older than me and therefore eligible only his hair's rather greasily lank, his complexion clashes with the sharp stripe of his shirt and he's tightly strapped into his waistcoat. I can't place him on any social scale that I recognise except that I think he's a Cambridge grad which puts him right beyond my ken. I'm almost engaged to G but still very alert to eligibility. Though like much else, I've got this badly wrong because Michael is gay.

Actually everyone here is socially beyond my ken. That's because I'm bourgeois to the rubber tips of my high heels and I've never known the likes of this lot. My parents – plumber's son, tailor's daughter – are working class people who have climbed gauchely into the middle class on the money ladder. We know about class. We haven't two cents of culture to rub together.

But the books – every kind of book – that line the entire wall of the Literary Department's large room, are classless. They arrive in great quantities from every publisher in London. They come with letters claiming the brilliance of the writer, the importance of the book and the publisher's sincere wish to see it reviewed in the pages of *The Sunday Times*.

It's my job every morning to list all the books that arrive in a big ledger – title, author and publishing date – and then to stack them on the shelves. There's no order. JWL will look through the recent arrivals and pick out those destined for notice. Slowly those not reviewed will move back and back and back until the shelves are so full that someone comes to clear them away, or Roy Thompson himself sends a minion to collect a few shelfulls. He doesn't mind of what. He orders them by the yard. We three, JWL, MR and me wince at this but as Sir Roy is our lord and master, we wince privately.

Not only does no-one mind me reading, no-one minds if I take a few neglected volumes home. My father can hardly believe it. He doesn't read more than a newspaper himself but he's impressed by these free perks of the job. In fact bringing home these free books is the first thing I've ever done to impress him.

He starts asking for the sort of book he can send as Christmas presents. I oblige. There's any number of them that look good but which no-one would want to read.

JWL is a very benevolent boss. He has a romantic, slightly theatrical look – that's because he's an expert on drama as well as literature – with soft, floaty grey hair and sometimes a bow tie. I recognise he's what you call 'distinguished'. He dictates his letters fairly slowly, tasting his words as he goes and finishing with a flourish. The letters go out to various eminent writers asking if they would like to review such-and-such a book. Sometimes JWL gives me manuscripts of poems or short stories to be sent back with a rejection slip. I add a letter telling the poor rejected author that he/she is wasting his time because *The Sunday Times* doesn't publish anything they haven't asked for or isn't by someone already well known. They shouldn't feel badly.

We have quite a lot of visitors in the Literary Department. Our two chief reviewers are Raymond Mortimer and Cyril Connolly. They're both very old or in Raymond Mortimer's case, very very old. He comes in to read the proofs of his review, donning a green eye-shade to do so, as if he's a reporter in an American movie. He has more wrinkles than anyone I've ever seen and appears to be stained brown all over. He hardly notices me, but I enjoy his voice which also seems stained brown and strong like stout, though it's the chain-smoking that's done it. I've no idea that I'm in the same room as someone from the Bloomsbury set who knows people like Vita Sackville West and Lytton Strachey and has had his portrait painted.

At least Raymond Mortimer can type which is more than Cyril Connolly can do. Mostly Conolly sends his hand-written review on the Monday morning train from Sussex and someone is sent to collect it. It's an anxious time waiting for Connolly's review. When it does arrive – written on headed notepaper – it's given to me to type, or rather to decipher his handwriting. I think that apart from reading the books, typing Connolly's review is part of my education

Sometimes he appears in person, review in hand. He's round as a ball, pug-faced and balding and so pasty it looks as if he never goes out of doors. He's a walking exemplum of what my parents feared might happen to me if I didn't get my head out of a book and get on my bike. He also looks as *sad* as a pug, mournful and melancholy and wanting comfort. He does say hello to me and sometimes pats my shoulder, probably because I'm necessary to him. To my young eyes he's so unprepossessing, so like a spoilt, sulky child, that I can hardly believe it when I learn he's on to his third wife and even less am I aware that I'm in the same room as the man who began the famous literary review *Horizon,* who is a great traveller, a lover of women, wine, food and beauty and whose apercus like 'there is no more sombre enemy of great art than the pram in the hall' will make it to the *Oxford Dictionary of Quotations.*

That particular apercu is not one I like, hoping, as I do, to one day have a pram in the hall myself. But I can well understand why he has written 'Imprisoned in every fat man a thin one is wildly signalling to be let out'. And I do feel sorry for him on that count and try to imagine the thin man wildly signalling to get out of his tubby frame. I don't much like the titles of his books – *Enemies of Promise* and *The Unquiet Grave* – and it's years before I read either.

I'm writing a novel myself. It's a kind of take on *Alice in Wonderland* crossed with St Augustine's *City of God* in which a girl is accompanied everywhere by a photographer on her journey to the City. Which makes it sound a lot better than it is.

JWL is always very kindly to Cyril as he calls him, and tries to cheer him up even though it's fairly obvious Cyril doesn't want to be cheered up, that's he's made something of a career out of witty melancholy. JWL knows this too so he doesn't try too hard.

My favourite visitor is the music critic Felix Aprahamian. He's short and plump with a goatee beard but he's as cheerful as Connolly is miserable. This is probably because music is better for your health than literature. Felix swishes in, beaming. He goes to concerts in a black, scarlet-lined opera cloak. He tells us, with glee, how he gets a railway compartment to himself by drawing his black cloak about him and pulling down his hat and looking so alarming that no-one wants to share the compartment with him. He does more than notice me. He gives me press tickets for the proms.

Years later, when I have a Robert Louis Stevenson fellowship that takes me to Grez-sur-Loing, near Fontainbleau, the village where Delius lived, I find that Felix, who adored Delius and became advisor to the Delius Trust, had been there years before me.

Another regular, diminutive and tubby visitor (culture doesn't seem to keep you slim) to the Literary Department, and whose shape seems to suit his name, is the theatre critic Harold Hobson. I seem to remember him in a bowler hat, black coat and specs that look too big for his face. He too can type or maybe his mother does it for him because he delivers his copy on a Friday afternoon, which is worryingly late for a Sunday paper but then he's been at the theatre on Tuesday, Wednesday and Thursday so has to write his piece very quickly. I've hardly ever been to the theatre. I'm unaware that HH is the critic who championed Harold Pinter's *The Birthday Party* when everyone else railed against it. Or that he's championed playwrights I'll come to revere like Tom Stoppard and Beckett.

(The things I'm doltishly unaware of, my head in a book at my desk in the Sunday Times Literary Department are, when I look back, horrifyingly legion. And the main one is that I don't realise that I'm at the very heart, the hub, of literary London and no girl was ever given a greater chance of belonging to it.)

I think Harold Hobson is shy, because he doesn't linger or else he goes next door to see Leonard Russell.

Leonard Russell is the Literary Editor and there's an adjoining door from our room to his. I've no idea what he does in there because his secretary, Stella Frank, keeps him closely guarded, hardly opening the door much beyond a crack when she wants to speak to me and he's in situ. Stella must be in her fifties or sixties and treats LR as if he was the king of England. In her time, she's typed letters to everyone from Enid Blyton to Evelyn Waugh with Aldous Huxley, E. M. Forster, Graham Greene and Robert Graves inbetween. Leonard Russell has passed most of the reviewing work to Jack Lambert and taken on the serialisation of important books like Montgomery's memoirs. Presumably once he's got one on the go, he doesn't have to do much, unlike us in the room next door, filling the review pages week after week.

Like Harold Hobson, or Hobson as I remember him, I'm shy too. I'm too shy even to notice when people like me which, in retrospect I think they did. I don't make any friends at *The Sunday Times* though there must be other young secretaries and shorthand typists all over the place. The only one I know, Gillian, belongs to William Rees-Mogg whose office is along the corridor from the Literary Department. I think Rees-Mogg has something wrong with his mouth which seems permanently pursed so I can't understand what he's saying.

Gillian is a few years older than me. She has a County look as if she's left her green wellies at home. She appears both ultra efficient and too busy ever to say hello. I'm astonished when she gets engaged to Rees-Mogg who seems stuffy and old quite apart from his pursed mouth and because I thought secretaries marrying their bosses only happened in *Woman's Own*. Certainly I don't suggest that she joins me for lunch which I have at the Gray's Inn Road transport café across the road from *The Sunday Times* building. I sit on a stool with a book and eat poached egg on toast and feel totally at home.

Thursday is the day when the book review pages are made up. Michael does it. He has mock-ups of the pages with the column pencilled in and spaces left for headlines and by-line. He does it standing up, the big pages spread out on his desk. Michael collects the reviews, including the one I've typed for Cyril Connolly, from the printer. They come in long strips like pieces of cloth, the print still wet enough to smudge. Once they're read, edited and corrected, it's jig-saw time. Scissors and smelly glue time. Time to consider the look of the page, where a picture might help, what headline to add and in what type. It's fun. I'd love to have a go but Michael never suggests it.

Michael's the Now (i.e. this Sunday), JWL is the future (Sundays to come) writing to authors asking for a review in two or three weeks time, planning the pages for a month ahead, sending the latest batch of crime novels to Julian Symons, novels to Frederick Raphael or Julian Jebb. We stick to publication dates because that's only ethical.

After I've been in the Literary Department for about a year, JWL sends me to interview a novelist called Jennifer Dawson who's recently won a prize for a book called *The Ha Ha*. He only wants a couple of paragraphs but he puts my initials at the bottom of it. And at Christmas time, when there's a big round-up of books, I'm given some to write about. A few more paragraphs.

Does this go to my head? What possesses me to leave the Literary Department? Why don't I stay on until I've read all the books on the shelves, become chief reviewer with five published novels to my name and a pad in Bloomsbury or Chelsea (Connolly's Chelsea to Mortimer's Bloomsbury) and find a vagrant artist to marry?

Is it that I want to leave home? Is it that I want to escape marriage to G? Is it that I can't look a gift horse in the mouth, that I am incapable of seeing anything straight and constantly come at life squint?

Whatever the reason, when I learn that Thomson newspapers have an indenture scheme whereby bright youngsters can train as reporters on one of the provincial newspapers, I decide to apply. In one of the many burrows of *The Sunday Times* I meet John Gay Davis who runs the scheme.

'I've written a novel,' I tell him.

'They all have,' he sighs.

Still, within a few months I'm en route to *The Western Mail* in Cardiff leaving behind the car my father's bought me as a twenty-first present and for which I care as little as I did for the bicycle he bought me at twelve, but taking my brand new portable Olivetti typewriter and keeping G. on hold!

During the next forty years I take two university degrees, I write umpteen children's books and several vols of poetry. My life is books, books, books. But those early days in *The Sunday Times* Literary Department when I was given the freedom to read and felt like someone given the freedom of the city, remain among my happiest memories.

The Author, 2011

SPOOKY SPARK

'Wonderful gossip!' said a member of the Royal Society of Literature after hearing Muriel Spark – 'one of the most elusive big cats in the literary jungle', as Philip Howard of *The Times* described her – reading from her recently published autobiography *Curriculum Vitae* (Constable).

Gossip about the dead, I wanted to add, and mainly about dead members of The Poetry Society. Not dead poets, you understand, but dead committee members, aspiring editors, bribing contributors, all those 'utterly abnormal people' who made Spark's two years (1947–9) as Secretary of the Society and Editor of *Poetry Review* an 'ordeal' she seems unable to forgive or forget.

'I like to think of them turning in their graves', she said with the sweetness of one of her own fictionally demonic characters. They might well have risen out of them as Spark went through her hit list: contributor Alice Hunt Bartlett ('pages of… rubbish with a cheque for twenty-five dollars'), committee member Robert Armstrong ('physically and morally twisted'), aspiring editor William Kean Seymour ('a born mediocrity'), Howard Sergeant, who spoke of integrity and compassion, but 'had neither', and vice-president Dr Marie Stopes – 'I was young and pretty and she had totally succumbed to the law of gravity without attempting to do a thing about it.' Two portraits of Dr Stopes were propped up against the platform. It's a wonder we weren't asked to stick pins in them.

But what possessed Spark to read this bitchy and tedious extract (concerned as Paul Bailey remarked on *Kaleidoscope*, with a writer 'settling old scores') to members of the Royal Society of Literature? I had the uneasy feeling that lurking in Spark's mind might be the notion that the living members of the Royal Society resembled the dead members of the Poetry Society, and I thought again of Bernard Levin's comment about her as the 'belle dame sans merci' who, if she had been born a few centuries ago, 'would certainly have been burnt as a witch.'

Curriculum Vitae (the title alone is worrying when one considers how one edits one's own) is a disappointing autobiography. It ends in 1956 when her career as a novelist really began, but I doubt if anyone will have high expectations of volume two. Reviewing this volume for *The Financial Times*, Isabel Quigly wrote, 'there is a lack of candour about almost everything important ...a mass of detail, trivia, self-justification and petty retrospective revenge.' One paragraph is given to Spark's conversion to Catholicism (in 1961 she published an interesting essay about it in *Twentieth Century*). 'She writes about her (ex) husband the way people talk about the milkman,' said Paul Bailey, 'and worst of all, almost nothing is revealed of the writer's passion for her work. One or two reviewers have praised her 'restraint', her resistance to 'the vulgarities of her age'. As a great admirer of her novels, I felt cheated.

There were moments in reading *Curriculum Vitae* when I wondered if Spark's intelligence only functions in fiction. Is she being naïve when she tells, in the preface, of her resolve – 'to write an autobiography which would help to explain, to myself and others: Who am I' – and then does no such thing? Or is she fooling us, playing with our expectations as she does so brilliantly in her novels? As a writer who knows more about the terrifying border lands between fact and fiction, the tricks memory can play, the human habit of making up the stories of our lives, how dare she risk the temerity of 'perhaps we should all write down our reminiscences to keep us from straying from reality in our latter days'?

The only satisfactory way to deal with *Curriculum Vitae* is to read it alongside the novel in which The Poetry Society features as 'the fictional background'. *Loitering with Intent* is written as the fictional autobiography of a girl called Fleur Talbot who, as secretary of the Autobiographical Association, spends half her time livening up the dreary memoirs of the members with a dash or two of fiction and the other half writing a novel in which she creates – or do they already exist? – the lives and characters of members of the Association. 'What is truth?' asks Fleur, 'I could have realized these people with my fun and games with their life-stories…' *Loitering with Intent* explores the nature of fictional and factual truth and in the way it communicates a writer's passion for writing, it tells us more about Muriel Spark than does *Curriculum Vitae*.

An unnerving feature of both books is that they end with almost the same phrases – 'I go on my way rejoicing' (LWI) and 'I …went on my way rejoicing' (CV). The phrase, used as a refrain throughout the novel, is borrowed from Cellini's autobiography. In *Loitering with Intent*, the autobiographies of Newman and Cellini are constantly held up as models. *Curriculum Vitae* can't hold a candle to either. The most interesting statement in Spark's autobiography is that she thinks of herself 'as predominantly a poet'. She has said this before, though no-one has paid it much heed and it will be a while before I can forgive John Mortimer (in the chair at the RSL) for resting on information gleaned in his 1988 interview with Spark, and not, while on the subject of The Poetry Society, asking her about her poet-self.

Someone did ask her why she had written a book about a novelist so different from herself as Emily Bronte. *Wuthering Heights* is that rare 'sport' the poem-novel and it was clear that Spark doesn't think of herself as different from Bronte as her questioner supposed. There was, she replied, 'a certain spookiness' in her own work. I suddenly remember all the haunting of a typical Spark novel, all the demonic characters who, put together, might make a Heathcliff.

Is she a poet first? Her novels have the quality of the fable and in each there is a poetic meditation on a theme, the Wordsworthian one of the growth of the child's imagination in *The Prime of Miss Jean Brodie*, old age and death in *Memento Mori*, suffering and the Book of Job in *The Only Problem* and over and over again, the way we betray our selves – and perhaps God.

What of the poetry itself? Spark has published two volumes, both out of print. The second *Going up to Sotheby's*, provides some interesting insights into her work. 'Created and Abandoned' has the narrator worried about the 'people of my dreams …limboed there where I left you forever like characters/in a story one has started to write and set aside?' 'Are you all right?' she asks them at the end. 'Against Transcendentalists' shows an 18th century rationalism with a touch of Stevie Smith:

What is Truth true of?
And what good's a God's-eye-view of
Anyone to anyone
But God? In the Abstraction
Many angels make sweet moan
But never write a stanza down.
Poets are few and they are better
Equipped to love and animate the letter.

Well, there was the unangelic Spark at The Royal Society of Literature, dressed as exquisitely as her fiction, dishing the dirt about the dead and fending off questions about God and the Devil. I went on my way rejoicing that she's alive, sparky, spooky – and still writing.

Poetry Review, vol no 3, 1972

UP WITH THE LARK(S)

Skylarks haven't been the same since Ted Hughes. For readers of the future, Shelley's 'blithe spirit' and Wordsworth's 'pilgrim of the skies' will have faded into the ozone layer, their symbolic associations with dawn and hope, joy and inspiration, lost forever. Hughes's bird, a creature 'Crueller than owl or eagle' will reign supreme.

Children (if skylarks aren't extinct) will not think of them singing 'at heaven's gate' but 'Scrambling/In a nightmare difficulty/Up through the nothing.' It is all very sad. It is also a very simple way of comparing how poets of the nineteenth and twentieth century think about poets and poetry. You want the ideology? Consider skylarks.

In particular, consider Shelley's 'To a Skylark' (1820), Wordsworth's poem of the same title (1825) and Hughes's 'Skylarks' (1967). Perhaps, for good measure (or the last of hopefulness) one should add Isaac Rosenberg's 'Returning, We Hear the Larks' (1917). Skylarks, in this poem, could be said to be on the turn between centuries. No post-war lark could sing, like Shelley's, 'of rapture so divine', or when the airways are so crowded, enjoy, like Wordsworth's lark, 'a privacy of glorious light'.

In Rosenberg's poem 'Death could drop from the dark/As easily as song' and the sweetness of the larks' song is somehow suspect. It is compared to a girl's kisses 'where a serpent hides'. That it should be song, rather than death, dropping from the skies represents not pure joy but pure chance.

All four poems seem to be part of a conversation between poets. There are points on which Shelley and Wordsworth are in agreement. For both poets the skylark represents divine inspiration. Their larks are mystics pouring upon the world a 'flood/Of harmony' (Wordsworth) or 'Singing hymns unbidden,/Till the world is wrought/To sympathy with hopes and fears it heeded not.' (Shelley).

Shelley's lark, famously bodiless, is all 'blithe spirit', Wordsworth's an 'ethereal minstrel' and, though it keeps an eye on its earthly nest, we are given no physical description of the bird. No 'shadow of annoyance' ever came near Shelley's lark. It has no knowledge of pain; it knows love but not 'love's sad satiety'; it knows death but also something about death 'more true and deep/Than we mortals dream'. It is all gladness and 'harmonious madness'.

One can imagine Wordsworth, firmly earthed in the Lake District, reading Shelley's poem and saying 'now, steady up a bit'. For while Shelley seems to imply that the skylark scorns 'Hate, and pride and fear' (and, by implication, all worldly matters), Wordsworth, asking his lark the rhetorical question 'Dost thou despise the earth where cares abound?' comes back with a clear 'no'. Even while the skylark's wings 'aspire', its 'heart and eye' are both with its nest 'upon the dewy ground'. Indeed the last lines of the poem could well contain a moral message directed expressly at Shelley.

> Type of the wise who soar, but never roam;
> True to the kindred points of Heaven and Home!

There are echoes of Shakespeare's 'Hark! hark! the lark! ' and of both Shelley's and Wordsworth's poems in Rosenberg's lines:

> But hark! Joy – joy – strange joy.
> Lo! Heights of night ringing with unseen larks:
> Music showering on our upturned listening faces.

Here the music is still something *given*, a grace dropped like manna, a source of joy.

All this is changed by Hughes's toughly bodied macho bird, 'barrel-chested for heights', its head like a whippet's, its body 'Leaded/like a bullet'. Some faint echo of Shelley's lark, compared to a 'high-born maiden/In a palace-tower' can perhaps be found in Hughes's use of the word 'towered'. 'A towered bird, shot through the crested head/With the command, Not die/ But climb/Climb/ Sing/ Obedient as to death a dead thing.'

The skylark's musical ease, the way in which in Shelley and Wordsworth its song *pours* forth and in Rosenberg's falls *showering* on the 'upturned listening faces', is gone in Hughes's poem as is the idea of an easy 'unpremeditated art' or an 'instinct more divine'. For Hughes's skylark, singing is a painful procedure.

> I suppose you just gape and let your gaspings
> Rip in and out through your voicebox
> > O lark

And the song itself is no longer one of pure joy. Rather, it is 'incomprehensibly both ways–/Joy!Help!Joy!Help! This seems like an explicit voicing of the death-or-song conflict in Rosenberg's poem.

Flight too is incredibly difficult for Hughes's bird. None of that soaring and singing of Shelley's lark in the 'golden lightening/ Of the sunken sun'. No floating and running 'like an unbodied joy' for Hughes's lark. His bird labours, 'Its feathers thrash, its heart must be drumming like a motor'. When it does get up there it doesn't so much sing as squeal and gibber and curse (up there in the madhouse that is heaven, being sucked empty by the sun, with all the other larks). Afterwards, when the larks have battered 'their last sparks out at the limit', when the 'agony' is over, they take the 'plummeting dead drop' down to earth.

Let no-one think that writing poetry is an easy or pleasant occupation. It's pain and sacrifice all the way and the only satisfaction of the profession is to feel something like various soldiers of the Allied Forces kept telling the TV cameras they felt – 'Weightless,/Paid up,/ Alert,/ Conscience perfect'.

But perhaps the most disconcerting quality about Hughes's poem is the altered cosmology. The skylark's song is no longer a given grace from above, rather 'The lark begins to go up/ Like a warning/ As if the globe were uneasy'. Hughes's bird is not there to bring us intimations of immortality or anything like. The lark-poet is a ruthless bird of prey. Its prey is the poem. It cares about nothing else. (It is, of course, a relative of Hughes's Hawk and Crow, of his single-minded genius Thrush with a brain like Mozart's). In contrast to a society's notion of the poet sent on his poetic flight of fancy to retrieve heavenly instructions (via a little divine madness), Hughes's larks are 'Like sacrifices set floating'. They are 'The cruel earth's offerings/ The mad earth's missionaries'. Martyrs all.

'A skylark wounded in the wing', wrote Blake, and 'A cherubim does cease to sing.' But the twentieth-century sky of Hughes lies 'blank open' and there are few enough people who have even seen a skylark – let alone a cherub.

References
Ted Hughes, 'Skylarks', *Wodwo* (Faber, 1967)
William Wordsworth, 'To a Skylark' *Poetical Works* (OUP, 1981)
Percy Bysshe Shelley, 'To a Skylark', *Selected Poetry and Prose* (Signet, 1966)
Isaac Rosenberg, 'Returning, We Hear the Larks', *Collected Poems* (Chatto 1979)

Critical Survey, vol 4, no 1, 1992

THE STORY LADY

A diary of the first two months of a residency based in the palliative care Alexandra Unit of Dumfries and Galloway Royal Infirmary.

Monday, October 20, 1997

Back in July, when I came for an interview, my first impression of the hospital was of a kind of ice palace, set on a hill, set outside town as though in itself it was contagious. Arriving in autumn, I find the place surrounded by the most lovely trees, all changing colour.

I've a week of meetings. Today Dr Lindsay Martin, consultant in palliative medicine, introduced me to the staff of the Alexandra Unit, which is to be my 'home base'. It's up on the top floor. Small – though it is the focus of specialist palliative care from Dumfries to Stranraer – six-bedded, a view of the Galloway hills and a serene, away-from-it-all atmosphere.

A roomful of strangers to face – doctors, ward sisters, staff nurses, Macmillan nurses. Found myself defensively taking out my notebook, at which they all looked slightly alarmed as if I was about to burst into poem.

Re-read the aims of this residency. The first one being 'to help patients, their families, carers and hospital staff to use writing to articulate their thoughts and by so doing to understand their condition and situation.'

'Understanding one's condition and situation' could take a lifetime.

Thursday, October 23

Busy getting lost in hospital corridors. The sister in Haematology told me a lot about leukaemia patients – particularly the story of B who died at the age of 41 and made a scrapbook of her life for her children. Leukaemia patients apparently have long periods of isolation. It felt like an area where I might be helpful.

The oncology liaison sister – she sees patients when they are first diagnosed as having cancer – talked of how different each patient was in their reaction to a diagnosis and how a period of denial can vary in its length or perhaps never be worked through.

The poem/story post box – my bright idea of a month ago, before I arrived – is to go up in the entrance hall plus a poster encouraging staff interested in writing to get in touch.

Sunday, October 26

At the suggestion of the chaplain, I meet Pete Fortune. Pete's brother, John, is dying. He's only 52, thin as the proverbial rake. Cancer – and a broken arm. He sleeps a great deal, disconcertingly with his eyes open. I think the Lord is looking kindly upon me making my first 'client' a professional short story writer. Pete arrived with three stories he's been writing about his brother. Mixed in with Pete's distress is something I recognise all too well – the need to write about it, the guilt at doing so, the desire for a reader. Brought the stories home. All three are powerful, moving, disturbing.

Monday, October 27

A first patient and a first poem today! E in the Alexandra Unit, who started talking about her best friend with such a natural rhythm that it was easy for me to write it down within the shape of a poem. E told me of her friend who, if she knew you were lying ill, would be 'up at the toot' – a rather charming expression which I took to mean the Scottish equivalent to the 'drop of a hat' – only nicer. I took it home to type up.

Wednesday, October 29

Saw Pete again. His stories deal with so many issues – a difficult family relationship, the fear of cancer in the family, the horror of cancer, not knowing how or if to talk about death – that I'm sure other people going through the same experience and reading these stories would feel, if not comforted, less lonely. Told Pete so and asked if I could keep the stories for the collection the hospital hopes to publish at the end of my year here.

Went to the neighbouring hospital, the Crichton Royal, today to find Rachel Mimiec, the artist in residence there. A young, warm and lively Glaswegian, she has an entire unused ward for her studio! And a piano.

Friday, October 31

Pete's brother died yesterday. I think he 'slipped away'. Certainly he seemed to be asleep most of the time.

Gave E her poem. She was terribly pleased with it and has been showing it to the nurses. She goes home tomorrow.

After living for all of 10 days without a full-length mirror, today I gave in and bought one at Argos. Felt quite excited about seeing my whole self again. And maybe now I can be 'wholly' here and a little less disorientated.

Monday, November 3

Meet Hector in the Alexandra Unit. He has arthritis and lung cancer. Found him in the unit's sitting-room smoking a cigarette (allowed if you tell the nurse and ask for the air conditioning to be switched on). He told me about his time as a shepherd. Hector's face, when he talks, is as lean and keen as a sheepdog's. Wrote down what he said and promised to bring it back to him typed up. His daughter has brought him a new pair of slippers. Now he has three pairs and a Zimmer frame.

Searched for a sheep poem among the 50-odd books I've brought with me thinking that maybe I'd be soothing a fevered brow with Wordsworth. Found a couple by Norman MacCaig but not quite right. Wish I'd brought Ted Hughes.

Tuesday, November 4

'What d'you want from me today?' asked Hector when I arrived in the Alexandra Unit. Said with a twinkle in the eye. I suddenly realised that he likes somebody wanting something from him. I suppose it's obvious really. Patients in hospital are constantly done-unto, with nobody needing something from them.

Gave Hector the first draft of his story. He began to remember all sorts of things he'd left out. His dog! The 'corbies' sitting on the dyke, the 'swish' of a big adder 'rolling in a circle like a bicycle wheel'.

Hadn't realised how invaluable would be the shorthand my father insisted on my learning in those far-off days when my ambition was to be a concert pianist.

Called into the Rehabilitation Unit today. Daunting. Two young patients with brain injuries who can't speak and several men who have had a leg amputated. As a smoker I live in as much fear of having a leg lopped as I do of lung cancer. A sight that gives me shivers is a hospital porter wheeling two amputees at once. It looks like an awful version of a nanny with two children in push-chairs.

Went into Orthopaedics and chatted to a farmer waiting for a hip op. I can imagine him on his farm looking tough and strong. Here, in his op gown, he looked small and scared. 'I've seen the vet at work,' he said.

Friday, November 7

Invited to Cresswell, the maternity hospital to meet the midwives.

There's a 'Quiet Room' at Cresswell. It must be one of the saddest rooms in the whole hospital. It's where parents come when a baby dies and where they keep an 'In Memoriam' book. Babies don't die. They are 'born asleep'. They are given names. They are given poems calligraphied in silver and decorated with a lamb, teddy or angel. There's a 'beloved daughter', 'a wee brother for Susan', a first born 'more beautiful than we ever imagined'.

Hector's going into a hospital nearer his home. He's given his shepherd story to his grandsons. Introduced myself to W a new patient in the unit who talked about his childhood in the East End.

Tuesday, November 11

W has got very enthusiastic about writing (me scribing) his autobiography. He was quite rude to his sister when she came visiting, more or less telling her he was busy and she should come back later.

Visited T who's had a stroke and can't speak. But I'm told he can write a bit. Had to quell the do-gooder's fantasy that I could break through his prison of silence by getting him to write reams. But he's a man who looks more interested in football than words. Took him Nick Hornby's *Fever Pitch* in the hope he might be sparked.

21

Wednesday, November 12

W's autobiography. He's 40 and married. Yesterday his sister brought in a photograph of him as a young man. 'Weren't you dishy!' I said. Got a big grin.

The poem/story post-box is now in situ.

The canteen is hard going. Lunchtime is groupie time. Twelve consultants will cram themselves round a table meant for six. Sometimes I find another solitary being and sit by him/her. Yesterday a woman from the accounts department who says, 'We thought you might be here to help people write their wills.'

Took comfort in rhubarb crumble.

Thursday, November 13

The archivist at the Crichton Royal Hospital showed me round their museum. They have the art work and case histories of psychiatric patients from 150 years ago. My favourite is a beautifully executed tri-lingual playbill done by a patient 'separated from the world for five years, much of which he has spent rolled up in a carpet and prostrate on the floor.'

Monday, November 17

W died early this morning. We'd finished his autobiography, though the last thing he said to me was 'I haven't told you about when I was a gold smuggler…' In retrospect it seems a wonderful last line. I think his body was still in the ward and I wanted to go in and say 'goodbye' but didn't like to ask.

A new patient in the unit has asked me to write 'goodbye' letters to his family. It felt like the most important thing I've ever done. Had to keep back tears and concentrate on my shorthand.

Do I care more for a good poem than a patient's health? A

good poem is one spoken from the heart and surely that's health-giving? A rationalisation? And then fear, confusion, grief, doesn't come nicely shaped but all rough and disorderly. One frequent wail – 'It's not fair!' and the cliché, 'We've all got to go sometime,' said with total lack of conviction.

A meeting about an Arts Therapy evening, planned for the end of the month. Rachel is to talk about her work at the Crichton and I'm to give a reading.

Thursday, November 20

This morning a sister stopped me in the corridor to shake hands. 'What ward are you on?' I asked, all eagerness. 'Out-patients', she said. I don't know what I can do in out-patients but promise to visit.

In the Alexandra Unit a young wife has been keeping vigil over her husband for days now. We had a coffee together in the canteen and she wrote a love poem for him.

One of the sisters has suggested a patient who might like to see me. M is waiting for a worrying prognosis. She says she's 'coasting', watching silly television programmes, trying not to think.

Saturday, November 22

A seminar in Glasgow. The launch of Lapidus (the Association for the Literary Arts in Personal Development) in Scotland. The writer/carer conflict was one of the themes. John Killick, who works with dementia patients described 'scribing' for a woman when her son came in and began a blazing row. Should he have stopped scribing? The language was so powerful – 'All I'm interested in is my life's going' – that he wrote on.

Thursday, November 27

M has come up with a cracker of a poem. I gave her a first line and she was away, speaking it. She was very elated when I brought it back to her, typed. And so was I. Indulged (briefly) in the illusion that this one poem might change her life. The consultant arrived just as I'd given her the poem and she said 'Look! I've been published!'

The Arts in Therapy evening. A small but appreciative audience of hospital staff. Rachel and I came home afterwards and ate cheese on toast. Agreed that an essential quality of a writer/artist in residence is big teeth and a big smile. We've been asked to do a print exhibition of our work but decided it would be more fun to do something new together. A long corridor wall is used for art exhibitions. We could write/paint a poem on it. But will they let us?

Sunday, November 30

Weekend writing poem for wall.

Monday, December 1

Meet the two speech therapists. Much talk about 'swallowing difficulties'. Began to have difficulties myself due, I think, to a childhood memory of X telling me that if you swallowed a hair it would wind round and round your throat and you'd choke to death. 'If you're going to have a stroke,' says one of the therapists, 'try to have it on the right.' (Or was it the left? Anyway, one side affects both your speech and your writing hand. A double cruelty).

We've got the go-ahead for a poem on the wall!

One of the nurses in the Alexandra Unit sometimes introduces me to a patient as 'the story lady', a title I rather like. Easier than 'writer-in-residence'.

Wednesday, December 3

Ventured into Out-Patients yesterday. Chatted to several patients and told them about the poem/story box (which remains resolutely empty). Rather hoped the waiting time – written up on the board – might be something like three hours. That would be enough to drive anyone to write a poem, if one of protest. But it was only 30 minutes.

Despite the fact that I know that poems and poets appear in unlikely places/people, I couldn't bring myself to approach a phalanx of three stern, buttoned-up looking women. Probably missed a lyric or two.

Monday, December 8

Last week was a difficult one. Most of the patients in the Alexandra Unit have been too ill to see me. Or they talk lucidly on one day but by the next have suddenly become weaker and less coherent. I can't tell how much is illness and how much is the pain-relieving drugs. Disconcerting.

And timing a visit to a patient is so difficult. I need to avoid the doctor's rounds, the nurses' change-over time, lunch, visitors – not to mention the poor patient wanting to sleep! Sometimes it feels as if I have to 'catch' a patient while he/she is still well enough to talk but not well enough to go home – and that might be a very limited time of a day or two. It can feel rather predatory – trawling the wards for a poem or story.

Brooded rather miserably on this over the weekend but today had a long and helpful chat with Sister H about the drugs used. 'Nothing is given without a patient's consent,' she said. She also said that the last week or so had been a time of 'slow deaths' and it wasn't always like this. She made death sound something like birth, like when a woman hasn't quite come to 'full term'. A physical emotional and spiritual readiness.

Since I've been here there's been a patient who told her sons and the nurses she was going to die on Friday, and did. I'm not there to witness an actual death but people seem to die so quietly ... I think of Dylan Thomas's 'Do not go gently ...'

The staff of the Unit seem keen to have a writing workshop in the new year. Am encouraged.

Tuesday, December 9

Saw a patient suggested by Dr Martin. T has been very ill and the experience seems to have left her rather haunted and full of strange imaginings. Fascinating to the writer in me, though afterwards I thought it might be healthier to get her thinking about everyday affairs. Selfishly glad that she's a patient who might stay for some time.

Monday, December 15

Christmas decorations going up. The Rehab Unit looks like Oxford Street – or, as the sister said cheerily, 'a tart's boudoir'.

T is looking better. No need to worry about her being haunted. She's obviously back to her more normal, down-to-earth self. Slightly disappointed!

Another 'slow death' in the Alexandra Unit. P's wife has been sitting with him day and night. I asked her if she'd talk to me about this time of waiting and she agreed. 'I hope that's helped you,' she said afterwards, 'because it's helped me.'

Friday, December 19

A frustrating morning. E began to open up and talk about her childhood – dancing in the kitchen while her father played the fiddle. Shades of Laurie Lee, I thought, but I'd promised to visit another patient. E goes home tomorrow. I'll hear no more.

Sunday, December 21

Rachel and I spent most of the weekend painting the poem on the corridor wall.* Lots of comments as we worked.

'Cool!' (a group of lads).

'You need a full stop there,' (Auxiliary).

'Are you getting at us?' (A hospital porter reading the word 'loitering').

The spread of the words means that people read the poem out loud. Pleasing. Doors leading off the corridor serve as punctuation.

Noises off from X-ray. A child sobbing. Someone with an awful hacking cough. A few very alarming yells.

The nurses have started wearing tinsel round their caps. The joiner who made my (still empty) poem box told me he'd tried to make the box very discreet. It is!

Monday, December 22

One of the domestics, defending the poem-on-the-wall, has written a rude four-liner to a male colleague. Am pleased to have provoked this.

Thursday, December 25

Late last night we went carol-singing round the wards – a group of staff and children wearing reindeer antlers and tinsel haloes. Most of the wards in semi-darkness apart from the Christmas tree lights. Began with 'Away in a Manger' in the children's ward. Big lump in throat. Liked singing our way up the stairs as if the whole hospital was being aired by song. 'Tidings of comfort and joy'. I hope so.

* Poem for a Hospital Wall

> Love has been loitering
> down this corridor
> has been seen
> chatting up out-patients
> spinning the wheels of wheelchairs
> fluttering the pulse of the night nurse
> appearing, disguised, as a bunch of grapes and a smile
> hiding in dreams
> handing out wings in orthopedics
> adding a wee drappie
> aphrodisiaccy
> to every prescription.
> No heart is ever by-passed by Love.
>
> Love has been loitering
> down this corridor
> if highly infectious
> mind how you go. If you smile
> you might catch it.

Telegraph Magazine, 7 February, 1998

WRITING AS EXPLORATION

Based on a talk given to the British Psychological Society.

I'd like to start by telling a story about a story. It's a children's story, so you'll all have to regress a little and I must apologise for the fact that, so early in the year, it's a Christmas story. I've chosen this one because I felt it most exemplified the theme of this talk – writing as exploration.

The title is *Why Father Christmas was Late for Hartlepool* – a title with little selling power except perhaps in Hartlepool. The plot is simple enough. It tells of four old and rather battered toys who have been abandoned in an attic and who are waiting for a new child.

What I want to try and do is to look at that strange interplay between the conscious mind and the unconscious mind that seems to go on in the process of writing a story or a poem. For me the excitement of writing, the initial sense of exploration, is that I'm telling a story and waiting for that story to tell me something. If it doesn't do that, if it doesn't surprise me in some way, then it has failed.

Seamus Heaney, in an early poem from his first collection put this very well, when he wrote:

I rhyme
To see myself, to set the darkness echoing.

To set the darkness echoing involves putting the conscious mind to one side, which, as I'm sure you know, is no easy matter. The conscious mind – or my own – is an awful censor, a know-it-all, and the one who likes to be boss.

When I was thinking about the title I'd given myself for this talk, a small voice in my head said, 'what d'you mean, writing as exploration? Isn't that a bit grand? Don't you mean writing as *play*?' And I had a sudden flashback to my own childhood in which I spent a lot of time on the beach with my mother.

My mother would sit firmly fixed on a rug with the thermos flask, her stockings rolled down to her knees, and I'd be a few yards away digging a hole to Australia. Exploring, if you like, but in a rather safe way because I know my mother has an eye on me and should I, by any happy chance, reach Australia, she'll haul me out by my heels.

I think this is the nearest I can get to a description of the relationship between the conscious and unconscious mind in the process of writing – though I have to add that the conscious mind isn't nearly as reliable as one's mother. (I say this with a touching if idealistic faith in mothers.)

But let me get back to the attic and my four abandoned toys. I'm sure you will all have instantly tuned in to the word 'abandoned'. It's not a word I use in the story. I use the words 'left behind', because that seems to have much more of a wail and a sob in it than the word 'abandoned', which I think has an adult, clumping sound. You've only got to try the two out loud to hear the difference or to hear a mother in the street using that awful threat: 'I'll leave you behind!'

However, if I tell you that I wrote this story at a time when my daughter had left home for university and that the four toys were all real toys left in her attic, you'll begin to see that this story has some personal significance for me.

It seems idiotic of me to say that I don't recognise this at the time. I'm excited by the idea of four characters waiting for a child. It sets up echoes for me. I think of Beckett's *Waiting for Godot* and, rather gleefully, that I can re-write this for children and give it a happy ending! I've got four toys every bit as battered as Beckett's tramps and, it being Christmas, this waiting for the child is like the wait for the Christ child. These connections excite me.

In retrospect, I suppose the reason I don't recognise the psychological significance of the story for me is that I've distracted or tricked the conscious mind and somehow I've entered what feels like the Free Zone of play.

I think what this story tells the reader and what this story tells me, are almost certainly two different things. When the story is finished I experience what Henry James has described as the 'start that accompanies unexpected recognition'. And what I recognise, what the story tells me, is that I've been waiting, not just for my daughter to return, but for the little girl she used to be and that *that* child will never return. The story, though light and hopefully amusing, is, for me, an expression of loss. A kind of mourning.

Of course, I've known, with my head, that my daughter is now a grown woman and that she's truly left home. But somehow, by writing this story, I not only know it by heart, I've reached an acceptance.

You could say that the story has served as my therapist and actually it has treated me very kindly – more kindly than I would treat myself. If I'd been talking to myself about my feelings I'd probably be telling myself not to be silly and I'd do a fair amount of beating myself about the head on my mothering skills.

I recognise – again in retrospect – that my four characters are all aspects of myself. Of course they are! How could I blind myself to this at the time, but I do. Two out of the four have great problems with perception, with seeing. And of course this is literal as well as metaphorical. There's a one-eyed penguin and a rag doll who needs a good haircut to allow her to see properly. Knitted Owl is losing his stuffing – i.e. his memory – and Albapot, a china doll, is so clever she keeps tripping over herself, though the truth is she needs a new elastic band for her legs. In short, they're a bunch of inadequates but they're lovable.

Writing the story has done something else for me. It's allowed me to communicate how I'm feeling without revealing myself. I'm rather fond of Winnicott's description of the artist as someone who has 'the urgent need to communicate and the still more urgent need *not* to be found'.

My hunch is that there's that combined need in all of us. I'm talking now about the therapeutic value of the story to me and it has one last gift which is that it's taken me beyond autobiography.

31

There's a sense I get when I've written something that I feel is complete, that it's detached itself from me, that it exists in itself. It's like a bubble blown from a bubble pipe.

I suppose the thought I've been trying to reach in this talk so far is that thinking, feeling, expressing oneself by metaphor, simile, symbol is a very powerful way of 'setting the darkness echoing', of tapping in to the subconscious.

Having said that, I think most writers are wary of the idea of writing as therapy. There's a certain paradox at the heart of this concept. It's that writing is most therapeutic when it doesn't aim to be so, when that's *not* its purpose. How you, as psychologists and psychotherapists deal with this one, I don't really know. I think I'd suggest trickery. The kind of trickery writers use and which I've heard described as 'to catch yourself not looking'.

In addition, I think most writers are aware that writing can be a dangerous occupation. You may learn things you don't want to know. A sufficient number of writers have either gone out of their minds or committed suicide or both, for this to be fairly obvious.

Having struck this wary note and having described the way writing has been personally therapeutic, I'd like to go on and talk about the patients I worked with during my year as writer-in-residence at Dumfries and Galloway Royal Infirmary and to try and assess the therapeutic value of writing.

To give you a little background – I was working mainly with cancer patients, patients who were terminally ill, some patients, such as amputees, who were in the rehabilitation unit, and a group of disabled people as well as relatives and staff.

Let me give you the gist of two of the aims of the residency as set out in the job application form:

1. To help patients, families and staff to use writing to articulate their thoughts and by so doing to understand their condition and situation.

2. To create a body of writing which can be made available to foster greater understanding of personal responses to illness, death and bereavement.

Both aims, I think you'll agree, are exploratory and indeed the idea of the residency itself was an exploratory one. Can writing help? I think if I were talking to a different audience I would emphasise the very many ways in which I think it can – and did. Speaking to you, I'd like to talk about both the positive and problematical aspects of the work.

The therapeutic benefits of writing worked at a number of different levels and in ways I hadn't expected at all. For some patients writing about a memory of childhood was a distraction from present pain and distress. For some it was a way of re-assessing their lives. Some used writing to express anger or fear. Some – and this was perhaps the most painful part of my job – wanted to write goodbye letters. I think for many patients, writing helped as an affirmation of identity – something easily lost in hospital. And I think a number of patients enjoyed the feeling of being needed and valued which came with someone around wanting their thoughts or stories. They also liked being able to share these with relatives and staff. The idea that what they wrote might, when published, be helpful to other people, often served as a great incentive.

One of the most difficult parts of my job was introducing myself to patients. Of course sometimes one of the consultants or nurses would prepare the way for me, but often I had to start from cold as it were and introduce myself as the hospital's writer. Some patients thought I wanted them to report on the hospital and that made them feel very alarmed, because if you should complain, who knew what the medics might do to you? A few patients thought I wanted to steal their stories to write my own best-seller, and of course there was the macabre joke of the nurses that I was there to help patients write their wills.

Another problem was timing. Patients got better and went

home. Some died. In between they might be well enough to talk and write one day, but not the next. There were doctors' rounds, meal times, visiting hours – all things which made it difficult to establish a sense of continuity.

I think one of the original ideas of those setting up the residency was that I'd be able to accompany cancer patients on what they call 'the clinical pathway' – i.e. from diagnosis, to cure, to remission or death. This didn't really prove possible, not least because I don't think anyone wants a writer around at that awful moment of diagnosis. What I was able to do, was to build up a relationship with a number of patients who were in and out of hospital, or coming in regularly for chemotherapy.

There were – obviously there were – a number of patients who had not the remotest interest in writing anything. When I made the suggestion to one patient, that he might like to write down some of his thoughts, he looked at me very balefully and said, 'Well, your thoughts are your own, aren't they?'

In contrast to him was a man called Henry. He came from the borders of Yorkshire and Lancashire and told me very early on that he thought poetry was childish and he hadn't the slightest intention of writing anything. We did, however, strike up a rapport and he would tell me periodically that I was 'chipping at his armour'. I ended up writing a poem for him and he was terribly pleased with this and insisted I put his full name on the dedication. He planned to send it to all his friends, but in the event this was something his wife did after he died.

This is the poem:

A Poem for Henry who doesn't like Poems
(i.m. Henry Clement Smith)

Here's an invisible bunch of flowers.
They don't need a jug. Or water.
Keep them in your mind's eye

And they'll last forever. Look,

Here's Lancashire daffs, not lightly
Blown over and sturdy tulips, Yorkshire
Bred. The bougainvillea from Rhodes
Could warm the winter. But best of all

The roses that you've grown.
They have your touch, your fingerprint
In their petals. I've put in poppies,
Multi-coloured, frail, but with the knack

Of thriving in unlikely places –
Like a poem, in fact.

Although there were patients who didn't want to write, I rarely met one who didn't welcome a chat. In fact, I had to learn that just chatting was valuable, sometimes perhaps more valuable than writing. Because I'd been given the job of encouraging people to write, it was often difficult for me not to want a product all the time – what for you might be a 'result'.

Something else I had to learn was how to focus a patient on one particular topic. That topic usually emerged during a chat. Quite early in the residency I worked with a lovely man who decided to write – or to have me scribe – his autobiography. He got very deeply into it, to the extent that if his sister arrived he'd get quite rude to her because she was interrupting his flow. The whole thing took an enormous amount of time and I got very worried that he'd die before we finished it. But he didn't. It was almost as if he were hanging on until he *had* finished it. Almost. Because what, for me, was most touching, was that just before he died he said, 'I haven't told you about when I was a gold smuggler'. It was somehow just so splendid. Here was I left holding the facts of a life with this one thing – so dramatically appealing to a writer – missing. It was as though he died with some mystery still intact – and that pleased me.

But let me return to thoughts of writing as exploration. I think there was a big difference between generations. The older patients were often stoical and courageous, but they'd grown up believing that you kept your feelings to yourself. They were happiest writing about memories and of course there is an exploratory element in that. The younger patients were much more in tune with the idea that expressing your feelings is psychologically healthy.

The two groups of people whom I think found writing particularly therapeutic were relatives and a group of disabled people, with whom I had a regular workshop. Somehow relatives either keeping vigil, or who had just experienced a loss, could use writing to express grief. This is an example:

The Waiting

I don't want to leave him
Until he leaves me.
It's been two weeks now.
When he came to the hospital
We thought he'd be built up
And fixed up. Instead
He's gone down, down, down.

I've been here from nine
In the morning until nine
At night. Travelling in
And not knowing if
He'd still be here
Has been the worst.
Some nights I've slept here.

He's gone this distance
And I have to go
This distance with him.
I wish he'd die now.
My daughter says,
'Can't they give him something
To help him go?'
But they can't.

We've been married
Forty-five years,
I could have kicked him out
A thousand times
But he's the only man
I've ever loved.

Jenny Turnbull

One wife more or less commissioned me to write a poem about her husband, who had just died and whom I didn't know. It felt very odd, like being the village scribe and asked to write love letters, or whatever, and I was bemused by her notion that you could order a poem like you might a funeral wreath.

The workshop sessions were held with a group of disabled patients. I didn't use writing to explore disability, although some of the group did write about it. I treated it more or less as I would any group of writers and I think the therapeutic value was the sense of accomplishment and the sharing of thoughts and ideas.

It perhaps won't surprise you to hear that the most difficult people to wheedle any writing from were the medics – the nurses and the doctors! When I began working at the hospital I was innocently unaware of the hospital hierarchy. I discovered there was a considerable degree of nervousness, either about what I might write about them, or what they might reveal about themselves. It was very difficult to convey that idea, implicit in

Winnicott, that it is possible both to communicate and remain hidden.

With patients I always felt that I had to tread both gently and warily. Physical illness is often not the time when anyone wants to 'set the darkness echoing'. That darkness can seem all too close and frightening. Patients could be in any one of those emotional states often charted as anger, despair, denial. Few patients had the knack, either natural or developed, of thinking in metaphors, similes or symbols – which for me is such a therapeutic aid.

There was one man, a cancer patient, who was writing a thriller. I thought this was a brilliant metaphorical approach that I wouldn't have thought of in a million years. The story was about a man threatened by a mysterious killer.

Mostly I tried to let patients lead the way in what they wanted to talk or write about, very conscious that I didn't have any training in counselling or therapy.

This brings me to what, for me, is a problem I can't see my way through and which is perhaps as much a problem for writers working in health areas as it is for psychologists and psychotherapists. It is to do with that paradox I mentioned earlier that writing is most therapeutic when it is not treated as therapy.

An opinion on the art/therapy debate that I most favour is that of the American poet, Kenneth Koch. 'It is better to teach poetry writing as an art than to use it as some form of distracting or consoling therapy,' he writes. 'As therapy, it may help someone to be a busy old person, but as art and accomplishment it can help him to be fully alive.' This, I think, is the ideal. The reality is that distraction or consolation is exactly what many patients want and who would deny it them? These are valid, understandable needs that writing can satisfy. And although the resulting story or poem is probably not 'art', I've yet to meet a patient who didn't derive that sense of accomplishment referred to by Koch.

In part, my advantage within the hospital was that I wasn't a medic, I wasn't an authority figure. I never approached anyone with the idea of 'I am here to do you good'. I was interested in stories just as stories.

There have been any number of patients who began by saying, 'Oh, there's nothing interesting in my life' and who then went on to tell stories of love, war, travel, farming, exciting deeds, intimate family incidents.

Over the year, my post-box in the hospital's entrance hall collected a curious mixture of contributions – love poems, thank-you poems, poems signed and unsigned, poems on the backs of envelopes and once, a poem written on a paper bag by a mother with a child in the hospital.

As writer-in-residence, I was something of a cuckoo in the hospital nest. But the patients were the larks.

British Psychological Soc. No 26, December 1999

MEETING W. S. GRAHAM

I met W. S. Graham on an Arvon course at Totleigh Barton in 1979. The tutors were Edwin Brock and Jim Burns. Graham was the guest poet and I one of some fifteen or sixteen students. I was 38 and it was my first time away from my children and, from memory, the first time I'd had five days in which to do nothing but read and write poetry. By the time Graham arrived, with Nessie, on the Wednesday night, I was already high on the stuff.

I'd heard of Graham but had never read any of his poems. And so I was quite unprepared – 'undefended' – is the word that comes to mind – for the Graham persona, the Graham voice, the elegiac intimacy of some of his poems, his obsession with language. Of all poets, I think of Graham as the poet's poet.

With his sailor-blue eyes and his bushy brows (*'my eyebrows have whitened and gone rogue'*) he appeared like the reincarnation of *The Seafarer,* storm tossed, sea-washed. Even as I write this, I find myself thinking, irrationally, maybe he was! I think he was wearing what looked like a much lived-in suit, though it could be just that he seemed very at home in his body. And of course he was drinking whisky, and of course Nessie was keeping an eye on him.

What I didn't realise then, but know now, is that when it comes to poetry readings, I was in the hands of (under the spell of?) a master. For a start there was what Robert Calder, in an *Edinburgh Review* essay, called *'the beautiful parlando'* of his *'straightforward Scottish voice.'* Edwin Morgan, in possession of Graham's programme notes for a reading, found *'the margins spattered with handwritten commands to himself, almost in the manner of musical annotation'.* Graham was a 'performance poet' long before that term came into being and 1978–9 seem to be years in which Graham was much in demand as a reader.

There were no books for sale at Totleigh Barton and having now read *The Nightfisherman: Selected Letters of W. S. Graham,*

(Carcanet 1999) I understand why. *Implements In Their Places*, published in 1997, was out of print and Faber's *Collected Poems 1942–1977* didn't appear until the November of 1979.

This explains why I typed out, on my Olivetti portable, *To My Wife at Midnight* and a second unpublished poem which Graham read at Totleigh Barton that night. This was *The Musical Farmer*, a poem which was not included in the Collected. It was eventually published in 1990 in a Greville Press Pamphlet of *Uncollected Poems* – now out of print.

The morning after the reading, I found myself playing a Beethoven sonata on the grand piano in Totleigh Barton's barn while Graham listened. I don't remember how this came about. I was unaware of Graham's passion for music. I think he might simply have expressed a need to hear some. What was the order of the morning's events? Was it the pub (with all of the students) then the piano, or the piano then the pub? I don't remember either.

When I got home I felt I'd 'caught' Graham's voice, in the way you catch a cold and can't shake it off. I wrote to him and sent him some poems. He replied by return of post. His letter-poem perhaps needs little explanation, and if I have kept it to myself for over twenty years, it's because, in part, it represents a deeply unhappy period of my life.

Graham autographed my typed copy of *To My Wife At Midnight*, writing in brackets, under my name 'Tragedy-eyes'. I was rather flattered. I shouldn't have been. In a letter to Ronald Duncan, Graham confessed to a 'quick knowledge' of people. The editors of Graham's letters, Michael and Margaret Snow, quote Nessie as saying that 'he knew more about most people in five minutes than they knew about themselves.' Soon after that visit to Totleigh Barton I went through an episode of manic depression and soon after, divorce. Perhaps it was all prefaced in my then 'tragic' eyes!

The lines in Graham's letter-poem:

O have I spoiled everything
You really want to say

refer to the following lines from what I can only call a kind of 'mimic' poem of my own.

By the way, you will observe
you have taken over my voice.
Only for the time being, I hope
because that nice poet
with the blue eyes,
Edwin Brock – and you
may have given me
my own.

It will be obvious from Graham's reply that the George he refers to was then my husband. Mike was another student on the course, one equally enthused by Graham the man and Graham the poet.

I'd like to include Edwin Brock in this memory of Totleigh Barton. He and I corresponded for some time. Unfortunately, and probably because of the traumas of illness and divorce, I only have two of his letters.

In the last one, dated January 1981, Brock expresses his disappointment at not being taken more seriously by the critics and his desire to write a poem 'not out of guilt and despair and tensions' but 'out of some quite different emotion. I daren't say happiness because I don't think I'm capable of that. Maybe just negative capability.' His letter concludes with the sad remark, 'I'm no longer sure that I have a self I want to express.'

And so it was a particular pleasure for me to receive the posthumous volume *And Another Thing*, (Enitharmon 1999) and to read in the preface by Anthony Thwaite, that Brock experienced 'a final flowering' and 'a prolific phase of writing poems' that continued until he died in 1997.

In retrospect, I suppose that what both Graham and Brock tried to convey during that Totleigh Barton week was not only how to deal, in poetry, with intense emotion, but that almost impossible task of – in Graham's words – 'telling /Each other alive about each other/Alive.'

All these years later, I remain deeply indebted to both poets. Graham's letter-poem is a dear possession. I still smile to read his handwritten *'Cheerio, from now'*.

Dear Diane,

> I see your letter is lovely,
> Not bad, a kind of poem
> Sent to speak to me
> While I am in the middle
> Of hearing and old opera
> I like. Cavaleria
> Rusticana. (Take the d
> Out of and in line five.
>
> Oh have I spoiled everything
> You really want to say.
>
> Say nothing. Your Bristol
> walls are looking at you,
> Going away to indulge
> Yourself in Poet Scapes.
>
> Come on my deario
> What are you going to do
> At your good age now.
> Have you got George firm

As a dear love to put
Your arms round? He sounds
Maybe a good man who
Knows you. I'm maybe wrong.

I have the letter from Mike.
What you say about him

(watch out watch out watch out
Domingo is doing the great
On with the motley.) Were you
With me here earlier speaking
To Mike over the table
Or down in some weeks back
Putting out the best of my poems
Not for them but to help
Myself speaking. Now look
My dear if you've got anything (*get me up from the sore floor*)
        handwritten
From me me yo O I fell
Now. A scarlet stream
A thread of blood is showing
From the Scotch corner
Of my fierce mouth.

Cheerio. I can't write
    This very long. I send
    A kind of kiss. I send
    A kind of kiss for George
    Very unqueer hoping
    You will get the bedst out of him.

44

Look at the dusk of real night and my days
Moving in. Tell George I'll take him outside
And put the heid on him not for your sake.
Cheerio I must leave you now. I
Remember your face. Don't make anything of it.

Last three lines are handwritten and written sideways

Cheerio, from now

   Love, Sydney x

PN Review, vol 27, no 5 May–June 2001

IAN HAMILTON'S OBLIVION AND THE POET

The questions posed by Ian Hamilton in his introduction to *Against Oblivion* are those that nag at all poets – even, I suspect the Heaneys and Sweeneys of our times.

Hamilton was asked to write 'an updated, twentieth-century version of Samuel Johnson's *Lives of the Poets*'. It was to contain a mini-biography and mini-critique of up to fifty poets – dead poets, like Johnsons's, but poets who had enjoyed 'substantial reputations when alive.'

It was in the process of choosing his poets that Hamilton began brooding on the fact that of the fifty poets in Johnsons's *Lives*, he was only familiar with the work of half a dozen. Of the other forty-plus, some, like Thomas Yalden and Elijah Fenton had 'vanished from the map.'

Inevitably, considering his own list, Hamilton asked 'how many of my own poets would ultimately go the way of Johnsons's?' And what of the poets on his 'sub-list' – poets 'once admiringly reviewed … but now teetering on the edge of oblivion, an oblivion which presumably they had spent whole lifetimes seeking to transcend?' *Teetering!* The word is enough to give any working poet vertigo.

All the questions voiced by Hamilton hang on the word that's in the very title of the book. Is the driving force within a poet the desire for immortality? If so, considering the odds and remembering the lost Yaldens and Fentons, he/she could be on a hiding to limbo. Not only is poetic immortality a highly chancy business, depending, at least a little, on fashion and luck, but the poet may have a wholly deluded belief in his/her own gift.

Are these dreams of immortality which Hamilton describes as being central to the whole business of creative composition in the 18th century, still as compulsive today or have they been modified? I doubt that any poet today, aware of our celebrity culture, the publishing scene, the proliferation of poets, the shelf-life of books and the tremendous changes wrought by technology, can dream so sweetly as those of 18th century poets. Nevertheless, I suspect that the desire for immortality, though undercover, is as rampant as ever. And is it, after all, such a folly as Hamilton seems to suggest? Is it not, in an exaggerated form, the desire present in everyone, simply to 'leave a mark?' And though in its extreme negative aspect its consequences could be a wasted life, used constructively, could it not equally provide the impetus to produce the best possible work?

If, having stared oblivion in the face, you should try to comfort yourself with thoughts of possible fame, modest success, a single poem lingering on in an anthology, Hamilton can soon discomfort you. According to Hamilton, what the 20th century poet could no longer hope for, 'was the kind of central, civilizing social function for which …his gifts and insights so crucially equipped him.' Despite the fact that poetry did not take over from religion, poets continued 'to insist that what they had to offer was, potentially, of world-altering significance. In practice, the world did not have much use for them.'

So there's the poor poet, with no place in heaven and, it would seem, of little use on earth but somehow 'saddled' with the 'strange conviction' that he/she has been 'singled out for creativity' and still clinging to the belief that 'being a poet really matters.' Hamilton finds it poignant to contemplate 'whole lifetimes given over to a vocation for which the world in general has little use.' That a few poets are honoured and prized by the world only makes matters worse for the majority who then suffer a sense of 'cultural neglect' and 'professional exclusion' resulting in 'a kind of career envy.'

It is perhaps instructive to consider Hamilton the man, the poet, the editor, the critic, the biographer, in order to understand why his view of poetry and of the poet's life is so glum. *Against Oblivion* was written when Hamilton was suffering from cancer. He died before the book was published. Easy then to think that he was working on it while facing his own possible 'oblivion'. But in fact most of the thoughts found in the introduction inform his biographies (of Lowell, Arnold and the aborted one on Salinger) and his book on literary estates and biography, *Keepers of the Flame.*

What bugs Hamilton most is, at heart, a moral conflict. Does a great gift, such as Lowell's, give a poet the right to live his life in a way that is destructive of others, that is ruthlessly ambitious and dominated by egocentric vanity?

In *Ian Hamilton: In Conversation with Dan Jacobson*, Hamilton talks about his biography of Arnold and says that the question for Arnold was 'how to lead a poetic life without turning into a monster or without making terrible compromises that might sap whatever creativity he had...'Added to this is the 'debilitating stress' of wondering if you were any good at it in the first place or of discovering, half way through your creative life, that you weren't. It sounds like a nightmarish scenario yet I suspect all poets are afflicted with such anxieties and conflicts.

To Jacobson, Hamilton acknowledged that he was attracted to writing about writers he both admired and was repelled by. Jacobson suggests that Hamilton's engagement with such writers was due, in part, to 'a deep ambivalence about the activity of writing, as such, let alone about the nature of the persons who actually do it.' Hamilton replied that he certainly felt ambivalent about the 'airs and postures' and 'sky-high hopes' attached to writing. 'Think of whole life-times devoted to an objective that may be worthless because of a lack of talent anyway. And because it doesn't do anything...'

Apart from this last statement reiterating Auden's debatable dictum that 'poetry makes nothing happen', a key element of Hamilton's moral being resides in giving something to the world, being *of use*, of contributing to the common welfare of mankind. And this, in a way, seems to be at war with his undoubted passion for poetry.

In the late eighties, when Faber published Hamilton's *Fifty Poems,* Lachlan Mackinnon lamented the fact that 'shunting poetry aside' has left Hamilton so little work to show, suggesting that he could have been a larger, more influential poet. Perhaps the rigorous critic in Hamilton – so valued by many – worked against him, for in assessing his own poetry he 'he came to the conclusion that there wasn't enough in me to sustain a full poetry-writing life.'

Was he right or was it that he didn't dare risk it – the possibly wasted life? To decide to dedicate one's life to poetry is to risk wasting it. To attempt poetry at all is a risk. And are there not millions of seemingly 'wasted' lives and who is to judge them as such? Every aspiring poet must be familiar with those hours, days, weeks of wondering if one's time could have been better spent digging the garden or making soup. Here's T.S. Eliot, in 1942 in wartime London, working on 'Little Gidding' and writing a letter to E. Martin Browne:

> In the midst of what is going on now, it is hard, when you sit down at a desk, to feel confident that morning after morning spent fiddling with words and rhythms is justified activity – especially as there is never any certainty that the whole thing won't have to be scrapped.

Hamilton's focus on the 'airs and postures', the 'sky-high hopes', the 'tyrannical' quest for 'after-fame', doesn't take into account some of the many effects on an individual of attempting to be a poet. The attempt involves a study both of history and literary traditions, a striving for honest expression, a careful listening to oneself and others, a training in acute observation, a learning of craft and technique, a developing consciousness, a musical ear, the act of attention that Simone Weil likened to prayer – not to mention the battle with the demons of ambition, vanity and egocentricity. You may not become a good poet but you might become a better person. Alternatively you might end up embittered and disappointed though either way might be as much to do with temperament as lack of success. I am of the opinion that the art itself serves as a major antidote to the worst psychological faults and vices, for nothing can so wreck a poem as a false thought or feeling. And all this is not to forget the rewards – the absolute delight in sometimes producing a poem that is more than you are.

Perhaps, currently, there's a new zeitgeist. In a recent review of D. J. Enright's final book, *Injury Time: A Memoir*, Ian Sansom contrasts poetry's 'high road' which 'takes itself utterly seriously' and the 'low road' in which 'you understand writing as an aspect of wise living.' According to Sansom, apart from writing a lot of poems about death, Enright 'seems to have lived a good and truly lively life.'

But this still leaves unanswered Hamilton's contention that the world has no use for poetry, that it won't 'alter the world or make the world a better place.' I turn to the title essay of Seamus Heaney's *The Government of the Tongue* in which he comments on the letter from Eliot quoted earlier:

> Here is the great paradox of poetry and of the imaginative arts in general. Faced with the brutality of the historical onslaught, they are practically useless. Yet they verify our singularity, they strike and stake out the core of self which lies at the base of every individuated life. In one sense the efficacy of poetry is nil – no lyric has ever stopped a tank. In another sense it is unlimited. It is like the writing in the sand in the face of which accusers and accused are left speechless and renewed.

It is not enough to quote another's claim for the value of poetry. I'm left wanting my own testimony. Poetry can comfort, explore, disturb, lament, praise, surprise, delight, provoke thought, bear witness, companion you through almost all life's experiences, offer you something which, at its greatest, comes from something unconquerable in the spirit of humanity. How could we live without it?

Paradoxically, of course, it's clear from *Against Oblivion* that Hamilton couldn't. Excluding the four great poets he calls the overshadowers – Yeats, Hardy, Eliot and Auden – Hamilton chose forty-five poets as potential 'survivors'.

In part, *Against Oblivion* works as an anthology: every poet, apart from Plath (whose estate refused permission) is represented by one or two poems. It's easy to query the choice of poets and to plead for the doomed, as Anthony Thwaite did in his *Sunday Telegraph* review of the book, complaining about the inclusion of 'some not-very-good (or awful) American poets.' But this always seems to me to be a pointless exercise. However erudite, well-read and of sound mind an editor or anthologist might be, there is an inevitable subjective judgement at work and perhaps never more so than with Ian Hamilton who regarded 'a genuine poetic moment as miraculous, or near miraculous, akin to what I imagine might be the moment of revelation for a mystic.'

Against Oblivion is an immensely readable book, critically astute, wittily rude and written as if Hamilton is a kind of Apollo assessing the poets as they appear at the foot of Parnassus. He's refreshingly rigorous about it so that you feel most poets only just scrape in with 'could do better' written on their earthly report cards. Here are a couple of examples.

On Hughes's *Lupercal:*

...in the general enthusiasm few critics were ready to take note of the discrepancy between the poet's lively, expert eye for nature's detail and the crudity of most of his ideas.

On Frost:

Now and then Frost jawed on tiresomely and was always too fond of the cracker-barrel aphorism, but every so often he achieved an intimate, intense and yet forbearingly intelligent dramatic forcefulness...

These examples typify the Hamilton method of appraisal which is to balance praise and complaint, to set up and knock down or vice verse, condemn and redeem. John Carey, reviewing *Against Oblivion* in *The Sunday Times*, wrote that the book 'glitters with insights like flecks of mica'. This is true enough, though it has to be said that not all the glitters are kindly.

Aphorisms abound. Robinson Jeffers's work described as 'high-prophetic and low-readable'; HD charged with 'cosmic breathiness and fiddling narcissism'; Lowell's early verse defined as 'strait-jacketed hysteria'; Stevie Smith's religious conflicts described as her 'cute spiritual despairs'.

Well, you have to laugh, and quite often say 'yes, that's it exactly!' In an editorial in *PN Review*, Michael Schmidt contrasted two views of Hamilton. One has him as 'grudging... narrow impatient...' The other as 'exacting... rigorous... fearless... urgent.' Perhaps Douglas Dunn is closer to the mark, writing in an as yet unpublished elegy, of Hamilton's 'withering wisdom, tenderness, concern...'

For a quick and lively overview of 'Some Lives of the Twentieth Century Poets', *Against Oblivion* is just the ticket. Were I to recommend a book to someone approaching twentieth century poetry for the first time, this could be the one. Yet I'd want to add perhaps another two. Michael Schmidt's *An Introduction to Fifty Modern British Poets* for its breadth and because it includes the 'overshadowers'; and Heaney's *Finders Keepers: Selected Prose 1971–2001*, because Heaney seems to possess a greater generosity of spirit and never fails to acknowledge the poet's struggle. With Hamilton, you get no marks for trying.

It's perhaps unfair to contrast Heaney's full-blown essays with Hamilton's pithy appraisals, but a couple of examples would seem apt. Writing about Elizabeth Bishop's last volume, *Geography III*, Heaney speaks of 'a consciousness squaring up to itself and taking the measure of its own strengths and weaknesses.' Hamilton, commenting on the same volume, writes 'even the one or two late pieces of hers that have been called *confessional* are essentially well-guarded, wry, rueful and impressively resigned.' And, by implication, disappointing.

Then there's Hugh MacDiarmid. Presumably Hamilton only included MacDiarmid because he met the criteria of being dead and having 'enjoyed a substantial reputation' for he has nothing good to say of either the man or his poetry. His appraisal concludes 'better – perhaps – the fake Scots of this bad-tempered poet's youth than the prosy dreariness of his maturity.' Consider Heaney's account of MacDiarmid's later years, years in which 'he now endured the beginnings of an ordeal in his poetic being one in which the megalomaniac and the marvel-worker vied for the voice of the bard'.

But I'm carping. Hamilton's prose, critical acuity and wit are a delight. Few books of criticism can make it as bedtime reading. Hamilton's can. And my guess is that his work will survive at least until the next century.

The Dark Horse, Spring 2004

THE NECESSARY LIFE

Edwin Arlington Robinson: A Poet's Life by Scott Donaldson

About halfway through this biography, I'm struck by the thought that unconditional love by a biographer for his subject is maybe not such a good idea. Here's Scott Donaldson's opener. 'This book derives from the conviction that Edwin Arlington Robinson was a great American poet and an exceptionally fine human being.' Well, there's telling you. Somehow his 'conviction' has a defensive ring to it that sets up a kind of resistance, at least in this reader.

This is Donaldson's seventh literary biography – others include Hemingway, Fitzgerald, Cheever and MacLeish – but 'none of them' Donaldson writes, 'rank alongside Edwin Arlington Robinson as a human being.'

This is the first biography of Robinson for forty years. Apart from wishing for a clearer index and a chronology of Robinson's life, Donaldson's book provides a fascinating, thoroughly researched account of a poet's struggle against a great many odds – family tragedy, unrequited love, poverty, neglect and alcohol. Seven years in the making, *Edwin Arlington Robinson: A Poet's Life*, draws largely on a trove of more than 3,000 of Robinson's unpublished letters, a great many of them collected by the critic Wallace L Anderson and left languishing in a warehouse after Anderson's death.

Born in 1869, the third – and possibly unwanted – son of a prosperous merchant/ lumber dealer and a New England school teacher, Robinson grew up in the busy river town of Gardiner, Maine. Never a happy child ('I used to rock myself in a chair and wonder why the deuce I should ever have been born'), Robinson was an ungainly and poorly coordinated boy. When he was twelve a teacher, spotting him daydreaming in class, struck him under his right ear with the edge of her hand. It was a blow that caused almost total loss of hearing in one ear. How much this contributed to his lifelong reticence – he described himself as resembling a New England shellfish, 'probably a Maine clam' – is impossible to know, but it can't have helped.

Robinson's early years – from age 19 to 29 – were marked by a sequence of appalling family tragedies. Called home from Harvard in 1888 to look after his ailing father he soon found himself also looking after his elder brother, Dean. Dean, a doctor, treated himself for neuralgia with laudanum and returned to Gardiner in the grip of a drug addiction he couldn't overcome.

Herman, the middle Robinson brother, handsome, extrovert and seemingly set for success in banking and real estate, wooed and and won the heart of Emma Shepherd, the life-long love of his younger brother. Neither Herman's marriage (in 1890) nor his commercial success were to last. Alcoholic, he squandered the family fortune on reckless investments.

Donaldson describes the winter of 1896–97 as 'a season in hell' for Robinson. There was the slow and agonising death from diptheria of his mother, Mary. Dean had become 'a hopeless burden' and Herman was 'sinking into the grip of alcoholism.' In the family home at 67 Lincoln Avenue, there were now three brothers 'all addicted: one to drugs, one to drink, and the third to poetry' plus Emma and, now, her three small daughters.

Robinson became surrogate father (Uncle Win) to the girls but in 1897 was driven from home after a major quarrel with Herman. Returning home drunk after a fishing trip, Herman was helped into bed by Emma who then went to sit on the porch 'to collect herself.' Robinson, joining her, put his arm round her to comfort her and it was this scene which Herman, waking up, witnessed. Latent jealousy exploded and after raging at his younger brother an agreement was struck whereby Robinson, with an allowance, was to leave the house, show no further affection to Emma and give up any hope of one day making her his wife.

Given a job as a clerk at Harvard, Robinson moved to Cambridge. He resigned at the end of the academic year declaring that the post would 'make an imbecile of me if not a corpse.' 1898 found him back in Gardiner for the funeral of his elder brother,

Dean, aged 42. 'Apoplexy' was the cause named by the Gardiner newspaper, though suicide was suspected and is suggested in Robinson's poem, 'How Annandale Went Out'.

The events of this tragic decade – 1888 to 1898 – were to appear over and over in Robinson's poems about failed marriages, love triangles and love gone wrong. In later years, after Herman's death (of TB in 1909, aged 44) Robinson twice proposed marriage to Emma and was twice rejected although the bond of both family and friendship remained.

By 1899 Robinson was living in New York. With the family money gone, he was often poverty-stricken. Without a permanent home he was frequently dependent on the charity of friends either for money or a roof over his head. He seems to have been an off-on kind of alcoholic. There were sporadic jobs. A brief stint as a filing clerk at Harvard, another writing ads for a department store, nine months on the New York subway and, courtesy of Theodore Roosevelt, a clerkship in the New York Customs House.

Introduced to Robinson's poetry by his thirteen-year old son, Kermit, the president became a fan. Learning of the poet's poverty – and again urged on by Kermit – he resolved to find a way of helping him.

Apart from friends and the president's support, what really saved Robinson – both as a man and a poet – was the MacDowell Colony, an artist's retreat centre in Peterborough, New Hampshire. Robinson's first visit there was in 1911. It became his refuge. He wintered in New York and spent every summer at the Colony until the year he died – a total of 23 years.

Despite Donaldson's description of Robinson as 'an exceptionally fine human being' – a 'biographer of souls' in his poetry and a 'succourer of souls' in his life – I find it hard to warm to Robinson the man. Donaldson quotes Richard Cary's observation that 'for a taciturn, recessive man,' Robinson had an astounding number of close friends. He bound them to him, Donaldson writes, by giving each the 'distinct sense that they –

and they alone – shared a confidential intimacy…' and by offering, in times of crisis 'whatever advice, influence, and money he could muster.' Saul Bellow describes him as 'a world-class noticer'.

It's difficult to equate this with descriptions of Robinson as a man suffering 'a kind of helpless imprisonment within his own personality' or this by Elizabeth Sparhawk-Jones, a fellow Colonist, (her name sounds like a Robinson invention) who was in 'abiding spiritual love' with him – 'E.A locked the door on the inside, threw the key out of the window and thereafter couldn't reach it to let himself out.'

Robinson saw the role of poet as a semi-religious calling to which he was 'doomed, or elected, or sentenced'. To a friend from his Harvard days he wrote 'I want to give my whole life to the uplifting of others … but at the same time I want to be successful in literature'. Writing poetry was 'what he had been put on earth for'. Time and again, Donaldson writes, Robinson 'explicitly made the link between a life of poetry and a life of service.' If this all sounds uncomfortably priestly it's perhaps important to see the Puritan ethic at work in Robinson. As Geoffrey Moore noted in his introduction to *The Penguin Book of American Verse* – 'not the making but the message primarily concerned the Puritan poet.' (Somewhat unkindly, the editor, Malcolm Cowley wrote of Robinson that 'having taken vows of poverty, chastity, and obedience to his art, he could accept charity as if he were a whole monastic order.')

Enough of Robinson the man. What of Robinson the poet? His struggle to establish a literary reputation forms the most interesting part of this biography. Three years after leaving Harvard, Robinson claimed he'd accumulated 'one of the largest and most comprehensive' collection of rejection slips. His first book of poems, *The Torrent and the Night Before*, was self published in 1896. (The 300 copies arrived ten days after his mother's death.)

The book established both his style and subject matter. His

model was George Crabbe, the English poet who had demolished 'idealized pastoral' by 'describing with accuracy and sympathy the squalid, blighted, and eccentric lives of the poor folk of his native town.' Gardiner, Robinson's home town, became Tilbury Town, peopled with such unforgettably doomed or unhappy characters as 'John Evereldown' who though 'The shadows may creep and the dead men crawl,' is condemned to 'follow the women wherever they call.'

The book produced a number of good reviews and letters of praise but no publisher's offer. A second collection, *Children of the Night*, was published by the vanity press, *Badger of Boston*, the following year. It contained all but two of the poems in the first volume plus forty-three new poems, including 'Reuben Bright', a rare poem about a butcher and his reaction to his wife's death.

> And after she was dead, and he had paid
> The singers and the sexton and the rest,
> He packed a lot of things that she had made
> Most mournfully away in an old chest
> Of hers, and put some chopped-up cedar boughs
> In with them, and tore down the slaughter-house.

Also in this second volume was the now much-anthologised 'Richard Cory', that prosperous gentleman who 'fluttered pulses' and 'glittered when he walked.' This poem defines a key element in Robinson's work – the contradiction between the outer, public life or persona and the inner life. The portrait of Richard Cory – his wealth, his style, grace and good manners is built up through the first three stanzas. Those who see him think he has 'everything/To make us wish that we were in his place.'

Then, with his final stanza, Robinson cuts through all that has gone before, showing us that what we have seen of Cory has only been his public façade.

So on we worked and waited for the light,
And went without the meat, and cursed the bread;
And Richard Cory, one calm summer night
Went home and put a bullet through his head.

Louis Bogan described the book as being 'one of the hinges upon which American poetry was able to turn from the sentimentality of the nineties toward modern veracity and psychological truth.'

Publishing recognition was still hard to come by. Robinson's next book, a long blank verse narrative entitled *Captain Craig*, struggled for two years to find a publisher. It was eventually accepted in 1901 by *Small, Maynard* only for the manuscript to be lost by one of their staff in a Boston brothel. Fortunately the Madam preserved it. But by the time it was found, *Small, Maynard* had gone into receivership. *Captain Craig* was eventually published, though without much enthusiasm, by Houghton Mifflin in 1902.

Caught up in New York theatre fever, Robinson wasted a total of six years of his life (in two stints, one from 1905, the other from 1911) on unpublishable novels and unactable plays before he gave up on 'literary gallivanting' and settled for poetry.

At last, in 1910, *Scribner's* accepted *The Town Down the River*, the volume that includes the wry, semi-autobiographical poem, 'Miniver Cheevy'. Miniver loves 'the days of old,' and sighs 'for what was not'. The poet himself can surely be recognised in the fourth verse –

Miniver mourned the ripe renown
That made so many a name so fragrant;
He mourned Romance, now on the town,
And Art, a vagrant

The last two verses, reveal Robinson's self-deprecating witty self-awareness.

Miniver scorned the gold he sought
But sore annoyed was he without it;
Miniver thought, and thought, and thought
About it.

Miniver Cheevy, born too late,
Scratched his head and kept on thinking;
Miniver coughed, and called it fate,
And kept on drinking.

The Town Down the River was New York and the volume was dedicated to President Roosevelt. The poems were based on historical figures, family and some of Robinson's bohemian New York companions. A tribute to Lincoln opened the book, one to Roosevelt closed it.

In 1916 came the longed-for breakthrough with the publication of *The Man Against the Sky*. The volume included 'Eros Turanos', the poem thought to be based on Emma's unhappy marriage to Herman Robinson – 'She fears him and will always ask/What fated her to choose him'. (The critic Yvor Winters called it 'one of the greatest short poems in the language.') The *New York Times Book Review* gave the book an unusual amount of space, comparing Robinson to Dostoyevsky and praising the 'penetrative power' of the poet's vision. Amy Lowell in *The New Republic*, described the poems as 'dynamic with experience and knowledge of life.'

By now Robinson was a regular at the MacDowell Colony. His 'poetic energy reached its peak in his early fifties,' writes Donaldson. Four books were produced in two years. *The Three Taverns* and *Lancelot* in 1920 were followed by *Avon's Harvest* in the spring of 1921 and the Pulitzer prize-winning *Collected Poems* in the fall. *The Man Who Died Twice* won him a second Pulitzer, and *Tristram,* the third of his long narrative poems based on Arthurian legend (now rarely read or rated) won him another and almost became a best seller. (Conrad Aiken didn't share the enthusiasm remarking that the introspection of Robinson's heroes made them resemble 'helpless Hamlets.')

By the time of his death, in 1935, (aged 66) Robinson was regarded as the nation's leading poet. 'He was the first of our poets to write about ordinary people and events,' writes Donaldson. 'No one before his time would have thought it possible to write sonnets about an honest butcher consumed by grief, about a miser with *eyes like little dollars in the dark,* about ancient clerks in a dry goods store measuring out their days like bolts of cloth.'

In the last seventy years Robinson's reputation has waned. The New England crown passed to Robert Frost and Robinson's work was further eclipsed by the modernists, Eliot, Pound, Stevens and William Carlos Williams. It was Williams who posed the question 'Where does Robinson belong in American literary history?' Should he be considered the last of the 19th century New England poets, or rather, as Williams believed him to be, 'the great progenitor of the modern in its best sense.'?

In 1977 Geoffrey Moore claimed that 'Twentieth-century American poetry begins with Edwin Arlington Robinson.' In his 1998 *Lives of the Poets,* Michael Schmidt described Robinson as a 'transitional figure comparable to Hardy in all but scale and stature'. By 2002 he's an also-ran in Ian Hamilton's list of 50 poets who stand a chance of escaping oblivion. So taking into account the way a poet's reputation can rise and fall according to the fashion of the day, how justified is Donaldson's desire for the 'restoration of Robinson to the American pantheon?'

It seems important to keep in mind American poets' struggle to find a purely American voice, having, as Emerson said, 'listened too long to the courtly muses of Europe'. Robinson certainly has what Moore calls 'the heart-note of American utterance' – the clear, sharp language shot through with vivid and poignant home-truths. He's a maestro of both the sonnet and the dramatic monologue. He fits our century in that much of his work tells us that our only certitude lies in our incertitude and that we can hardly ever truly know another let alone ourselves.

Having said this, his range could be considered narrow and his over-arching themes of failure, disappointment and unhappiness are perhaps hard to take in an over-large dose. Frost (rivalrous, according to Donaldson) described him as 'the prince of heart-achers'. Yet for his understanding of the inner life of people, his poetry remains essential. Frost has a far larger range and a much greater sense of landscape. In much of Robinson's work one rarely escapes the confines and ethos of small town America. Also, despite the brilliant control of form, Frost's voice has a relaxed ease about it, missing in Robinson's more rigid control. Perhaps, in part, this is due to the fact that there is a strong 'I' in Frost's work, a sense of Frost the man, or his poetic persona, speaking to the reader. When Robinson uses the first person, it remains a detached voice. As Robinson said to an admiring young poet (Winfield Townley Scott) at the MacDowell, 'Don't go looking for me in my poetry, because you won't find me … Of course the mood, the thought, but you won't find me.' What you do find is Robinson's compassion for and ability to identify with the people and the lives he writes about.

The ranking of poets, the ups and downs of reputation, can be a spurious business. I'm in agreement with the British editor and critic, John Lucas, who, Donaldson writes, told a class of American undergraduates that despite the 'sadness of incommunicable isolation' to be found in Robinson's work, the poems escaped desolation through the affection in the poet's voice and through his fascination with 'the mysteriousness of people, no matter how ordinary they may seem.' This was what made Robinson 'one of the necessary poets.' I like that. Edwin Arlington Robinson – a necessary poet. Necessary in that his was the true democratic American voice moving into the 20th century to write of how extraordinary were the lives of so-called ordinary folk. After reading Robinson and absorbing his psychological insights, you can't walk the streets of your home town without considering those you see and wondering, wondering about their inner lives.

The Dark Horse, Winter 2007–8

POETIC SCIENCE

(A talk given to chemistry students at the University of Edinburgh)

A year as a Royal Literary Fund Fellow based in the Chemistry Department of Edinburgh University has made me ponder the connections between science and poetry and to wish to juggle with the common perception of the two being somehow in opposition. A sweeping generalization might be that poetry's *Fancy* and science *Fact*. It's now fifty years since C.P. Snow, in his famous Rede lecture, *The Two Cultures* (1959), outlined what he saw as the breakdown in communication between science and the humanities. It could be argued that like the Berlin Wall, the cultural divide came down a long time ago – if it ever truly existed. But what I'd like to suggest is that what *does* exist, and indeed has grown, is a language barrier that is intellectually limiting.

Let me here attempt to act as a kind of marriage guidance counsellor looking at the relationship between science and poetry. Why a marriage? Because science and poetry are bonded by their root in wonder and transformation. And why the need for a counsellor? Because they're a couple who seem to have drifted apart.

There are two books that have prompted many of my thoughts on this marriage of unlike minds. The first is entitled *Contemporary Poetry and Contemporary Science* edited by Robert Crawford of St Andrews University. The book is a result of the pairing of scientists and poets who met and responded (or not) to each other's work. The initiative for this came from the Sciarts scheme run by the Wellcome Trust with support from the Arts Council of England.

I'd like to quote you an extract by Eric Priest who holds the Gregory Chair of mathematics at St Andrews. He was paired with the poet John Glenday. Here's what Eric Priest said. I should perhaps tell you that his research interests include Solar Magnetohydro-dynamics.

Stimulated by observations of the sun, lots of ideas are continually floating around in my conscious and subconscious mind, and occasionally, when I wake up in the morning or am walking in the hills or working in the garden, one of them will take on a life of its own and crystallize. I then know in general terms the way I want to go but have to spend many weeks discovering the detailed steps, using all the skills and mathematical techniques at my disposal and often I will be led in unexpected directions on my journey to a fuller understanding. Indeed, the creative process of making poetry for John seemed very similar, including the initial spark of inspiration, the hard work (often taking a couple of months!) and the sense of the poem taking on its own life.

Among the other poets and scientists paired were the American Chemistry Professor (at Duke University), Warren S. Warren, and the Irish poet Paul Muldoon. This was the short poem Muldoon wrote after their meeting. It deals with the age-old poetic topic of the betrayed lover gazing into the loved one's face, but this time there's a scientific twist.

Once I Looked Into Your Eyes

Once I looked into your eyes
and the only tissue I saw through
was the tissue of lies
behind everything you do.

Once I looked into your heart
and imagined I could trace
the history of the art
of deception in your face.

Now there's something more than a chance
of making molecules dance
I'm somewhat gratified to find

that by laser-enhanced
magnetic resonance,
if nothing else, I may read your mind.

At a more personal level, one of the things that made me think
about the connection between science and poetry was an
invitation from Dr Jenny Rogers to observe an experiment she
was doing using the Vogenreiter Press. I have a limited
understanding of what Jenny was trying to achieve. I gathered
that she was attempting to synthesize a new material and that if
successful, one of its uses might be in wires that allowed electricity
to go through without leakage. Exploring electricity has, of
course, a very long and wonderfully exciting scientific history, so
that I see Jenny as working within an immensely long tradition.
This too is what a poet attempts to do – both to know and
understand the work of past poets, to absorb that knowledge into
his or her own work and then to make something new. One
might be unwise, for instance, to write a poem about a snake
without knowing D H Lawrence's famous poem simply called
'Snake' just as you might be unwise to launch out onto a
experiment without knowing what previous scientists have
attempted. One of my favourite descriptions of what a poem is,
comes from the American critic, Helen Vendler who wrote 'a
poem is a voice participating in a very long and very old
conversation about life.' Again, one could say the same of a
scientific experiment.

There *is* a difference though, in the use of tradition by poets
and scientists. It's a difference of perception. Poets think that
poetry changes, whereas scientists think that science progresses.
So science works by rejecting, or at least qualifying, the laws and
discoveries of the past – improving on what's already known,

working towards an ever-closer understanding of reality. *The Truth*. Poets, on the other hand, and perhaps less self-importantly, are merely offering another version of the truth, one that doesn't deny the truths of the past.

To return to Jenny's experiment – there was something else in learning about it that allowed me to make a connection with writing. The particular experiment I observed didn't work and Jenny told me that it 'might take 30 experiments to optimise the conditions for synthesis.' This reminded me of writing umpteen drafts of one poem. I hope this, plus the mental picture of a very full waste paper basket and perhaps, a drawer full of rejections slips, might suggest to you the unromantic aspect of a poet's work.

I'd like to refer back to that word used by Eric Priest and often used when talking of poetry: 'inspiration.' I think the equivalent term, for scientists, is the 'eureka moment'. Although I'd not deny either eureka moments or inspiration, the reality, certainly of a poet's work, is often much more mundane. Much of it, I think, is involved in preparing oneself by study and practice and thought for the possible and often rare moment of inspiration or, as the Scottish philosopher, John MacMurray, described it in rather calmer tones, 'a flash of insight.' I imagine this process is the same for scientists as it is for poets.

MacMurray wrote 'there is an aesthetic moment in scientific discovery, a flash of insight that fuses a mass of data and reveals the law of their unity, which is indispensable – even if this has to be 'subordinated immediately and strictly to the scientific demand for generality and experiment.' I think poets, concentrating on language, or exploring a subject, playing with it, trying it this way and that, might also relate to that term 'a flash of insight' and might consider a poem to be a thought experiment. A certain alarm attaches itself to words like inspiration and eureka moments. I think Seamus Heaney has written that quiet, intense concentration can release a poem as much as that flash of insight. One could equate this with Darwin taking more than twenty years to turn his flash of insight into *The Origin of Species*.

Another connection I'd like to make is that within the craft of poetry – in its metrics and forms and figures of speech – there is much that belongs to both mathematics and music and can perhaps be allied to the scientist's algebra and equations.

The second book I've been reading is *The Age of Wonder* subtitled 'How the Romantic Generation Discovered the beauty and terror of science' by Richard Holmes. This, as the blurb on the book jacket states is conceived as a 'relay race of scientific stories', a description that reminds me of Vendler's aperçu about a poem being a voice participating in a very long and very old conversation about life. Focusing on the 18th and early 19th century, the stories Richard Holmes tells are of Joseph Banks's expedition to Tahiti, William Herschel's astronomy/telescopes and his sister Caroline's comet hunting and, possibly of particular interest to chemistry students, the experiments of Humphrey Davy. What Holmes also brings out is the connection between these scientists and such poets as Byron, Keats and Coleridge. And what's worth noting is the number of scientists in this period and later, who also wrote poetry. They include James Clerk Maxwell, Humphrey Davy and William Rankine.

Of these scientists Maxwell probably makes the best poet. I'm much taken by the title of one of his poems – *Lines written under the conviction that it is not wise to read Mathematics in November after one's fire is out.*

Davy's poems, (he seems to have written poetry all his life) were published after his death, edited by his brother and given the somewhat unappealing title *Fragmentary Remains*. His book *Consolations in Travel* or *The Last days of a Philosopher* published in 1829, is described by Richard Holmes as perhaps the first ever scientific autobiography and stands alongside other memoirs of the Romantic age as Wordsworth's *Prelude*, Coleridge's *Biographia Literaria* and de Quincey's *Confessions of an English Opium-Eater*.

Here's a snatch of one of Davy's poems:

We trace analogies; as if it were
A joy to blend all contrarieties,
And to discover
In things the most unlike some qualities
Having relationship and family ties.

Thus life we term a spark, a fire, a flame;
And then we call that fire, that flame, immortal,
Although the nature of all fiery things
Belonging to the earth is perishable.

William Rankine published a book entitled *Songs & Fables* in 1874. Mostly he wrote light, but very lively verse. Here's a few lines from *The Engine Driver to His Engine*:

Like a train of ghosts, the telegraph posts go wildly trooping by,
While one by one the milestones run, and off behind us fly:
Like foaming wine it fires my blood to see your lightning
    speed –
Arabia's race ne'er matched your pace, my gallant steam-
    borne steed!
Wheel along, squeal along, sixty miles an hour!
Right through old England flee:
For I am bound to see my love,
Far away in the North Countrie.

My blessing on old George Stephenson! Let his fame for ever
    last;
For he was the man that found the plan to make you run so
    fast.

For both scientists and poets of this period there was a great exchange of thoughts and ideas. Davy organised Coleridge's first set of lectures at the Royal Institution. And here's Byron's comment on the times in the first canto of his long, satirical poem *Don Juan*:

This is the patent Age of new inventions
For killing bodies, and for saving souls
All propagated with the best intentions:
Sir Humphry Davy's lantern, by which coals
Are safely mined for (in the mode he mentions);
Timbucktoo travels; voyages to the Poles;
Are always to benefit mankind – as true,
Perhaps as shooting them at Waterloo.

What seems to have happened in the second half of the 19th century is that profession specialism within science somehow set it apart, or made it difficult, for that poetic-scientific dialogue to continue. In truth it has always been there. Edwin Morgan, Scotland's poet laureate and a poet who has tackled all manner of scientific topics from particle physics to the computer's first Christmas card, lists the links between poets and science from Lucretius, Dante, Milton, Goethe, Shelley, Virgil and Leopardi. One only has to think of the title of Lucretius's work 'De Rerum Natura' (The Nature of the Universe).

What of the current situation? Is there still an exchange between scientists and poets? Perhaps as in many a marriage the balance between lover and beloved is an ever changing dynamic. I'd like, a little nervously, to suggest that poets are more open to science than scientists to poetry. Poets seem to have tried to encompass science whereas scientists seem to have withdrawn from poetry.

Science gives to poetry new worlds to explore and in the main, poets seem pleased to take up that challenge. I'm less certain that scientists see the value of poetry, are willing to absorb the poet's leaps of imagination, the metaphorical ability (surely chemical at root) to combine unlikely elements and come up with fusion, not to mention the sharpening of the senses, the training of the eye.

Simon Armitage is a British poet whose range of subject matter includes global warming and astronomy. (Currently what is known as eco-poetry, poetry with a very particular concern for the environment almost has a genre to itself.) Armitage has suggested that 'poetry and science, for all their perceived differences, might well be attempting to accomplish the same thing through remarkably similar means,' though he points out that science is 'besotted with prediction' while the concern of poets is with possibility.

Here's one of his poems based on a science lesson at school in which he and another boy were asked to go outside and measure the size of the human voice. They were at a loss to know whether they needed a tape measure or a tape recorder, but in the event decided to shout at each other moving further and further apart. The distance between them when they could no longer hear each other would be the measurement of the human voice. This is the poem written much later.

The Shout

> We went out
> into the school yard together, me and the boy
> whose name and face
>
> I don't remember. We were testing the range
> of the human voice:
> he had to shout for all he was worth,

I had to raise an arm
from across the divide to signal back
that the sound had carried.

He called from over the park – I lifted an arm.
Out of bounds,
he yelled from the end of the road,

from the foot of the hill,
from beyond the look-out post of Fretwell's Farm –
I lifted an arm.

He left town, went on to be twenty years dead
with a gunshot hole
in the roof of his mouth, in Western Australia.
Boy with the name and face I don't remember,
you can stop shouting now, I can still hear you.

The lift-off in that poem comes when Armitage uses the measurement of memory to measure the range of the human voice. In an essay on poetry and science in which he refers to the poem, Armitage perhaps returns the subject to science, writing: 'They say that every sound ever made is still reverberating through the universe, however quietly and however distant.'

But perhaps among modern poets, the poet who has most managed to bring together poetry and science is the Czech poet, Miroslav Holub who died in 1998. Holub was an immunologist and regarded himself as a scientist first and a poet second.

Here's an extract from his dramatic and almost shocking poem about the moment of conception – what Holub himself calls 'the cellular stampede' in which the sperm meets the egg.

The last time
there was a genuine rampage,
herds stampeding
with the zest of hurricanes,
with the pulsations of a storm,
and the force of destiny,

that was when the sperm
made the journey
up the oviduct.
That was 'to be or not to be'.

Scotland's own Edwin Morgan has done much to present aspects of science with wit and humour in such poems as 'The First Men on Mercury' and 'The Computer's First Christmas Card'. (Nice to know this was written by a man who at 88 had only just acquired a computer, but never used it!))

Perhaps, as an aside, it's worth mentioning Simon Armitage's view that part of the role of poetry is not to be to be 'seduced, bewildered or fobbed-off by technology' and that, 'when double glazing, central heating screen savers and pot noodles conspire to disconnect us' poetry can be part of the campaign to stop reality becoming entirely virtual.'

But back to Edwin Morgan and the first of his six *Particle Poems*.

The old old old old particle
smiled. 'I grant you I'm not beautiful,'
he said, 'but I've got charm.
It's charm that's led me where I am.'

Opened up his bosom, showed me a quark.
It gleamed. He grinned like a clam. 'Sort

of heart, really, though I've got four.
They're in orbit, and what for

is a good question, unless to pump up
charm. I know I must look a frump
– just fishing – but seriously
would you not say I'm easily

the nearest thing to doom and centrehood
you've ever been unable to preclude?
Cathedrals – oh, antiquities and slime,
knucklebones, teeth five feet long, signs

and wonders, auks, knuckledusters,
twangs from armchairs, waters
waiting to break, cells waiting to squeak,
a sniff of freesia, a book

of hours, and hours themselves like days
in love, and even nanoseconds raised
by charm to higher powers, wait
until I make them, and fade.'

Shot off – never showed his age.

Sitting in on a couple of seminars given by postgraduates, I
found I hardly understood a word. But there *were* words which
for me were pulled out of their more familiar use and given, in a
chemistry context, a new meaning. Two such words were
promiscuous (applied, I think, to certain cells) and *chaperone*. (I'm
not sure what was chaperoning what). It made me think that if
words like this could be used as part of a scientific language, why
couldn't poets borrow words from the scientists' language?
Because scientists *have* a language. And one of the things about
learning a new language is that you also learn new ways of

thinking. Which is why, to me, an exchange between scientists and poets seems important.

John Herschel, the son of William Herschel who, by the by, apart from becoming an eminent scientists also wrote light verse and a translation of *The Aeneid*, wrote this about the word *iron*. There are those (the vulgar as he put it!) who 'regard this metal as incombustible, the chemist, who sees it burn with the utmost fury ...the poet, who uses it as an emblem of rigidity... the smith and the engineer in whose hands it is plastic... the jailer who prizes it as an obstruction, and the electrician who sees in it only an open channel of communication ...'

One word that carries a different meaning for different people. For me, if I'm able to allow that word to carry so many of those meanings, somehow my perception of it is enlarged. And in a small way, so is my perception – and indeed pleasure in – life.

Humphrey Davy said of chemistry : 'its beginning is pleasure, its progress knowledge, and its objects truth and utility.'

Robert Frost said of a poem: 'it begins in delight...runs a course of lucky events and ends in a clarification of life ...' Perhaps that 'clarification of life' comes close to Davy's truth and utility and brings poets and scientists together. Long may the marriage last!

I'd like to end with a poem of my own – for I've been trying to get just a little science into my own poetry.

Mr Obama and the Chemist
(for Neil Robertson)

After the chemist told me his plan
for catching sunshine
I went home with a dream in my head
of a mirror spread
across the Sahara, laden
with luminous dye and toggled

with solar cells. And I hugged
the hypothesis to myself
that one hour of trapped sunlight
could light and heat the world for a year
and was as cheered
as when Obama won the election
and wondered if I should write
and tell him about the mirror (black)
and the luminous dye
and the solar cells (cheap) and I began
to feel quite light-hearted & headed
as though at last I'd turned the corner
of twentieth century illness
and could hope
that my grandson
and my grandson's children
might be o.k.

Chemistry World, November 2009 (an extract)

MHOR CHANCE TO BE CREATIVE

At Moniack Mhor – Arvon's Centre for Creative Writing in the Scottish Highlands – the tutors are given rooms in a cottage just down the track from the main house. My room has all the charm of a log cabin, with a view of snowy mountains and a library on the ground floor. Gerry Cambridge – poet, editor, photographer and amateur ornithologist – and I are here to tutor ten Scottish and two Russian children, all of whom are winners of a Pushkin Prize.

This year (2013) is the 25th anniversary of the Pushkin Prizes, a writing competition for Scottish children aged between twelve and fourteen, twinned with a parallel competition in St Petersburg.

So why Pushkin? And why this Scottish-Russian literary alliance? The idea was the brainchild of Lady Myra Butter, a great-great-granddaughter of the Russian poet Alexander Pushkin (1799–1837), as a way of perpetuating her ancestor's memory. It began in 1988 as a small creative writing competition for children in Tayside and within ten years had expanded to include all secondary schools in Scotland. By 1993 it had made the connection with St Petersburg.

This year the ten Scottish finalists were chosen from more than 200 submissions by 60 Scottish schools. Pupils submit a portfolio of three pieces of prose or poetry. Judges in previous years have included some of Scotland's finest writers – Norman MacCaig, Douglas Dunn, Edwin Morgan and Anne Fine – and past prizewinners are now teachers, medics, politicians, writers, vets, physiotherapists and parents.

The Russian coordinator, Natalya Ushmanova, deals with submissions from the 37 English language specialist schools of St Petersburg. From a shortlist of ten, two have been chosen to join the Scottish children at Moniack Mhor for a week as the main part of their prize.

The aim is to allow the students to improve their writing skills and to expand and share their ideas in a week immersed in reading, writing and talking about books. It's about friendship and fun too. As Lindsey Fraser, one of two Scottish directors of the prize, says, 'Our prizewinners establish friendships that we hope will last a lifetime.'

Tuesday morning and Gerry takes the first workshop, in which he talks about list poems, personifications and kennings. The students can all have a go. David has been sick during the night, but he does his best with a list poem.

My workshop is on points of view and I ask the students to write 200 words about someone special to them. Then, for a bit of fun, I give them an exercise based on why the chicken might cross the road. (Point of view: chicken and one other.) They produce bandit chickens, chickens on a metaphysical journey and a weasel had up for chicken abuse.

In the afternoon Gerry and I do six one-to-one tutorials. Afterwards, Gerry takes the students for a walk.

That night, we're all to bring a favourite story or poem – either current or from early childhood. We get *The Hobbit*, some Harry Potter books, Enid Blyton and Norman MacCaig. One of the Russian girls, the extrovert Apollinaria, reads in Russian, then in an English translation. Her English is impressive: the other Russian girl, Maria, chooses to tell us why she loves Richard Bach's *Jonathan Livingston Seagull*. One Scottish student, Alisa, scores a hit with a reading from the picture book, *Where Are You, Blue Kangaroo?* Very soon we're regressing and joining in the refrain.

Over the week, there is an outing to Castle Urquhart and later a tools-of-the-trade session in which Gerry brings out his amazing collection of fountain pens. Their names make a lovely litany: Mabie Todd Swan, Wahl-Eversharp Skyline and Namiki Falcon.

Then there is his workshop about 'ways of seeing'. For my workshop, I pair up students and get them to discuss each other's pieces. I'm pleased with what David (now fully recovered) has written about Andy Murray and what Laura has written about her grandad. Gregor struggles with a piece about his father who died when Gregor was just seven years old. Apollinaria writes about her mother, who sounds incredibly glamorous.

The last night is ceilidh night. The girls have dressed up. Alisa, her hair in plaits, plays the flute. Apollinaria sings *Katyusha* with passion. Maria, who has been more introverted, relaxes at last, puts on a Harris tweed cap and sings a hippy song. Natalya reads Burns's *My Bonie Bell* and three of the girls sing *You Belong To Me*. It's one in the morning before we get to bed. The mist has rolled in over the mountains as if to say 'the show's over'.

And tomorrow it really is. There is a last morning workshop with all the students reading or performing something they have written that week. Lindsey collects poems and stories for the website (*www.pushkinprizes.net*). Hugs and email addresses are exchanged. No one wants to leave. But the coach has arrived to take us back to Edinburgh.

Will the students all carry on writing? Will they remember the advice of Lady Butter – 'You must have passion. Reach deep down'? Here's hoping.

Times Educational Supplement, 21 June, 2013

ASKING THE RIGHT QUESTIONS

The Earl Russell, O.M., F.R.S.,
Plas Penrhyn
Penrhyndeudraeth
Merioneth

30th December, 1964

Dear Miss McConomy, [my maiden name]

Thank you for your letter of 28th December. I am quite willing
to be interviewed for one of your 'profiles'. Almost any afternoon
at four o'clock would suit me, but perhaps you will telephone me
to fix a time.

Yours sincerely,
Russell

It was 1964 and Bertrand Russell, philosopher, mathematician, anti-war activist, Nobel Laureate was 92. I was 23, gauche, as yet unmarried and newly hatched from the news room when I was sent by the *Western Mail* (the national newspaper of Wales) to interview him.

The 'profiles' Lord Russell referred to in his letter were interviews with the eminent or famous, run under the wince-making title of *Feminine Focus*. If there was a slightly sexist edge to this, I was blissfully unaware of it. As far as I was concerned, to be asked to write the profiles was a gift.

This was my second of a three-year indenture scheme. The *Western Mail* was one of Lord Thomson's many papers and I'd got there via a secretarial job on the *Sunday Times*. I spent a year as a cub reporter in the Swansea district office. Swansea was a town I fell in love with, its streets as up and down as the Welsh valley voice, its beautiful Gower beaches, its Dylan Thomas hauntings. The office was small. The staff consisted of a rather handsome chief reporter, a lively young photographer, an ex-miner who could hardly breathe for pneumoconiosis, an elderly, very courteous man who'd been there forever and who reported on council and court affairs and an affable, warm-hearted Welshman who worked for the Press Association and who taught me to sing the Welsh national anthem in Welsh. I was happy.

And then I was called up to head office in Cardiff, allotted a desk in the features department (among the high-flying graduates who had the unenviable task of writing the daily leader column) and handed the gift of the profiles.

My reasons for wanting to become a journalist were probably all the wrong ones. I wanted to write. I wanted a cure for shyness. I'd left school at 16. Now I was a naive 23, full of conflict and curiosity, wanting a path through life. What became a year of interviews was akin to a personal university course. Hardly surprising then, that when I was given a say in the choice of interviewees, I managed to pick a philosopher, a poet, a painter and a comedian. Four life coaches, so to speak!

Yet looking through my old cuttings book, I see that the roll call of the good, the wise and the glamorous was amazing. Apart from Bertrand Russell, it included Sir Basil Spence, Harry Secombe, Stevie Smith, Brigid Brophy, Joyce Grenfell, Shirley Bassey, L.S. Lowry, Marlene Dietrich and Dora Bryan – plus a harpist, a parachutist, a headmistress and Alice Bacon, a Minister of State in the Home Office. Of all of these, it is Russell, Stevie Smith and LS Lowry whom my memory holds dear.

It was late January 1965 when I met Bertrand Russell at his home in the small Merioneth village overlooked by Snowdonia. Ushered in, I found him sitting in a wing-backed armchair, his hair as snowy as the mountains outside. My first impression was so shocking I couldn't admit it to myself at the time. Surely a 23-year-old woman such as myself couldn't be physically attracted to a man of 92, could she? Well, with his lean and aquiline features, that head that looked as if it could go on a stamp, that flyaway snowy hair, Russell was distinctly handsome!

Russell wants to talk about and promote his Peace Foundation, founded in 1963 (and still going). I want to talk about his book of popular philosophy, *The Conquest of Happiness*. We don't talk of conventional happiness. We talk of Russell's desire to learn more physics so he could 'decry nuclear warfare'. We talk of age, atheism and equality, with Russell saying that it will probably only be after a century of formal equality that women will have real equality. 'You know there have been times when women ruled the roost,' he says, '…that can happen again'. (Is there a twinkle in his eye?) What Russell most wants is 'equality of colour', predicting that it will be 'a long time – a bloody time – I mean "bloody" in the correct sense – before we get that.'

'Philosopher and rebel extraordinary' is the heading the sub-editor gave to my interview with Russell; it's a heading that could have been given to my interview with the poet Stevie Smith. What was surprising about Stevie Smith was the contrast between her small, seemingly insignificant personage and the provocative surprise of her poems, so many of which challenge Christian belief. She did so then, over lunch at Brown's Hotel in London (the place seemed full of vicars) saying, 'I think it better to have no God than a God of virtue. Man's greatest power,' she continued 'is the power to take his own life. Of course I wouldn't advocate suicide for any young person but I think old people ought to be able to make their own decision… I would think of it myself. They've taken the poison out of gas now, haven't they?' This last question tossed at me almost like a dare. I'm so agog, I've no memory of eating anything.

Stevie talks about her life with Aunt in their home at Palmer's Green. She began writing, she says when she was 23 'out of pain and suffering and the inevitable unhappy love affair'. (My age, I'm thinking – forget happiness, cultivate unhappiness). She says her most recent poem, 'November', took 55 drafts. (55 drafts! Should

I give up poetry?) I make a lot of notes – I have reasonably good shorthand –and type them up when I'm back in Cardiff. A week or so later she writes to the editor complaining that I got the colour of her eyes wrong.

Of all my interviewees, it is LS Lowry who most moves and charms me. He's so self-deprecating, and so funny and honest about being miserable. I meet him at his home, The Elms, a small stone house crammed with paintings and fourteen clocks each telling a different time. Currently, he's given up on industrial scenes and has turned to 'down-and-outs'. 'There are acres of them you know. Of course, when it's cold they don't come out, but on a nice day they come and sit in the park.'

They're happier than he is, he claims. 'I'm miserable most of the time…I get lonely. I think what if I fell downstairs and broke my neck. Nobody would care. And why should they?' About life itself, he sounds continuously astonished. 'I can't understand it at all…What's the point of coming if you've got to go? It's absurd.'

That he started to paint at all, was, he says, entirely due to chance. 'My mother and father looked at me with contempt. And then my Auntie Mary came along and all three looked at me with contempt. Then my Auntie Mary, bless her, said *What about the art college? He used to paint quite nice ships when he was eight.*'

Lowry eats all his meals out, so together we take a bus into town (I can't believe this is happening. I'm on a bus with a famous artist!) and have tea at … was it Lyons Corner House Café, or the Kardomah? What I *do* remember is Lowry's concern for the waitress. 'She looks tired,' he says. 'She's thinking about her pension.'

What I'm slowly discovering I suppose, is that talent – genius even – doesn't bring happiness.

So what of the others? Novelist Brigid Brophy who doesn't believe in heaven but does believe in Parnassus and would 'really like to know if Dickens is there'; Shirley Bassey who is at her best 'when slightly unhappy'; Harry Secombe 'once a goon always a goon'; Sir Basil Spence, 'I don't want to be greedy but I'm not satisfied with what I've done.'

And then there's the so-called scoop of an interview with Marlene Dietrich. September '65 and we meet at Liverpool's Royal Court Theatre. Dietrich stands posed on stage. Slinky gown, off-shoulder fur. She doesn't move. I'm kept looking up at her from down in the orchestra pit, asking questions she doesn't answer. I write a snooty piece. 'How long can a legend that has no story survive?' I ask, having quite failed to get *any* kind of story out of her. As if by way of an answer the newspaper includes a glamorous photo.

Perhaps the message to hold on to from my 'personal university course' is the one that comes from Joyce Grenfell – actress, singer, comedienne, writer and raconteur all in one – a woman who says she finds life fun 'because it's such a serious business.' Fifty years on – I agree!

Royal Literary Fund, 17 April 2017 (www.rlf.org.uk)

Reprinted in A Self Among the Crowd, Essays from the Royal Literary Fund's Collected Series, ed Gerry Cambridge, (Small Press Publishing, 2019).

LATE STYLE

It was alarming but exciting – a commission to explore. And on a winter morning in the Scottish Poetry Library we gave it the working title *Late Style*. Looking in the mirror at my 73 year old self, I thought *style* was probably all that was left and recalled a friend's mother who, at 90, took to cashmere shawls and a morning glass of champagne. The way to go, I thought. The way to go.

January 2015 and the three of us, three ageing poets – Douglas Dunn, Vicki Feaver and myself – had been asked to explore, in poems, age and ageing. What we wrote, we were told, was entirely up to us – be it 'four perfect lyrics or a 300 page verse novel.'

A commission's a wonderful thing tra la. It's akin to being desired. Somebody wants you, likes what you've done, wants you to do more. And joy of joys, is willing to offer both a generous fee *and* publication. It's also a terrifying thing. What if you can't do it? What if the muse pricks up its ears at the very word *commission* and makes for the door? And then the subject, age and ageing, was more than a little daunting. It meant looking back on one's whole life. It meant thinking about death. Ironically we had nine months.

I began a new notepad. A4 lined (for safety) yellow (for cheer). I rattled around in it as you would in an empty house. There were attempts at poems that fell flat on their noses. I ricocheted between two extremes – the grand one of wanting to write a contemporary version of Marvell's 'A Dialogue between the Soul and Body' – (*all that puff and bluster,* says soul, *you can hardly see yourself*) this petered out a few embarrassed lines later, and the other, more earthy option, my mother's teeth (*losing them was the end of youth*).

The first poem I wrote that made it into the collection of our poems published the following autumn by Scotland's Saltire Society – was sparked by Philip Larkin's *The Old Fools*, a poem that presents a grim view of the old *crouching below/ Extinction's alp*. But the lines that lit the match for my poem were *Perhaps being old is having lighted rooms/Inside your head, and people in them, acting.*

I recognised those lit rooms! Often, on the edge of sleep, or daydreaming in the bath, I hold an imaginary conversation with someone I know or have known. It struck me as as one of the pleasures of age to be able to live in both the past and the present.

Here's the poem.

Callers

> Well yes, maybe I *am* an old fool
> For there is a lighted room inside my head
> Where folk I know – alive and dead – come to call.
> It's like the foyer of a grand hotel,
> And though I'm out of sight I watch them all.
>
> Often it's my children, as they were when small.
> Yesterday a friend I haven't seen for years,
> My brother-in-law who died last spring,
> And a girl I used to know quite well at school.
>
> None of them stays long or knows they're here.
> I watch them look about then hurry on.
> It pleases me to think I might appear
> As guest or ghost in lighted rooms elsewhere.

I was exceedingly relieved to have written a poem that was relatively cheerful – or at least, positive. Have I mentioned my bi-polar disposition, my tendency to see cobwebs more than shafts of sunlight? I'm all too well aware that for some, old age is a ghastly business. I've seen stroke victims in hospital, known others slowly being worn down by debilitating diseases. I wanted to tell the truth without being either glum or gung-ho.

In retrospect, would I be cheered by the kind of minimal immortality offered by the end of 'Callers'? Maybe a little.

Although the idea of a contemporary version of Marvell's 'Dialogue' still lingers unfinished in the notepad, I was pleased when a dream provided the spark for a poem which is the closest I can get to some kind of belief. Lord knows I hate a poem or a story prompted by a dream! It seems such a cheat, though really one should just say thank you to the dreaming subconscious.

This dream was prompted by the haunting sound of a train going by in the night, a sound I remembered hearing as a child. And the poem that grew out of the dream was a kind of meditation on mystery. The yellow notepad recorded a favourite quotation from one of Emily Dickinson's letters – 'The unknown is the largest need of the intellect although for it we never think to thank God.' The need for mystery, the unknown, for whatever is beyond, became the poem that spread out in irregular lines across the page as if searching.

Beyond

Nothing so lovely as   the hoot
of a distant train
running through your dream.

                Is it childhood
you're listening to, worlds going off the map,
or infinity?

Always you liked views that spoke of beyond –
those seascapes stretching out that didn't stop at sky but went on...

What is it about the need for it? The why
of flight,   mountaineering the gift of grace.   How dire

if ours were the only galaxy!

How happily the word sits in the mouth, satisfying
as a communion wafer.

This is the sound of the distant train
running through your dream –

be-yond be-yond be-yond be-yond

One event that is certainly not so very far beyond, is death.
How to write about it? Death is something I've thought about
since I was eight, which was when my grandma died –
mysteriously disappearing so that I imagined she'd folded herself
up like a flower does at night and slid herself into one of the two
urns she kept on her windowsill.

Then too, I was a war baby. In a *Guardian* article, Colm Toibin
quoted Conor Cruise O'Brien on childhood and memory,
writing of how 'our elders have talked their memories into our
memories.' The stories my elders told, of Hitler and
concentration camps somehow merged in my childish mind with
the Sultan of 'A Thousand and One Nights' beheading a new wife
every night.

Now I'm of an age when there are more funerals than
weddings. Sometimes in bed at night I count my dead dears on
my fingers as if making a kind of rosary. I wondered if I could
write a long, long elegy that would include them all.

Then in April my sister died. I'm the youngest of three sisters,
Julie was the middle one and the one I'd been very close to as a
child. We'd shared a bed and I missed her terribly when she was
sent away to boarding school. But our lives took very different
routes and for the last twenty years I'd hardly seen her. The pain

of her death was an awful numbness, an inability to feel grief. The poem I wrote, 'Parting', was both an attempt to reach to a genuine grief by remembering the partings of childhood and to keep her memory alive. This is the first half of the poem.

Parting
(i.m. Julie Betty Rowan)

Early autumn the school trunk would re-appear
as if to say summer was over, time for my sister to disappear.

She was the homely one my mother loved too much.
A North Wales boarding school, my father's mute reproach.

Me – an avid reader of all Blyton's stories of St Clare's –
they kept at home, unaware I longed to go and envied her.

The trunk seemed huge, as deep as sorrow and in it
every vest and sock was named – only love went missing.

I remember most the heavy winter coat she had to wear –
grey as the railway station full of girls, grief in the parting air.

Apart from the prospect of writing elegies for my dead dears, I wanted to find some way of writing about my hypochondriacal fear of death. W H Auden's 'Twelve Songs' has one (the last one) with a jaunty rhythm and in which every verse ends with 'tell me the truth about love'. Could I borrow the rhythm to write a poem which might tell me the truth about death? The other poem haunting me was William Dunbar's wonderful growling Lament for the Makars, *Timor Mortis Conturbat Me* –the fear of death disturbs me – the line taken from the Catholic Office of the Dead. I couldn't, as they say, have put it better myself! So here's my poem with a salute to both the medieval Dunbar and the 20th century Auden.

Timor mortis conturbat me

Will it give me six months warning
Or come when least expected?
Will I trip over it one morning
And find myself disconnected?

Will it come on the way to Corstorphine
Or when sitting on the loo?
Will I need a lot of morphine
Will a bottle of brandy do?

Will it happen in broad daylight
Or wait until it's dark?
Will it come like a lover at midnight
On a necromancing lark?

Will I lose control of my bladder?
Will I lose control of myself?
Will the Lord send down a ladder
And shock the National Health?

Will it start as a minor chill,
Then turn to a nasty cough
Will it spread everywhere until
Someone has to switch me off?

Is it already growing inside me?
Does it have a date and a time?
Will I know when at last it's untied me?
O what's the use of rhyme?

During the nine months that we were given to produce those perfect lyrics or verse novel, Douglas, Vicki and I met up two or three times to share poems, sometimes lunch and once –

workshop's reward – time on the beach at St Andrews plus ice cream. (Second childhood comes to mind).

And of course part of the pleasure of exploring age and ageing was to read the work of others – Milosz's wonderful 'Late Ripeness', the witty grannies of Muriel Spark's *Momento Mori*, D H Lawrence's cheering belief that 'It ought to be lovely to be old/ to be full of the peace that comes of experience...'

Perhaps I might be helped to loveliness and peace by that morning glass of champagne. In a poem called 'End Matter' I listed the things I needed to say – sorry and thank you – and to do – bless and praise. A praise poem almost eludes me until one Sunday afternoon, when we go to see the swans and their new cygnets on the lake...

........it's an idyll: trees, shining water, new life,
grandly mythical swans, sunshine – all the ingredients
for a perfect praise poem. And then I turn my head

and see him, the heron, standing stock still in the watery
rushes, watching and waiting, blatant as death. The locals
say there were five eggs, now there's only one cygnet. I flap
my arms at him, shout to shoo him away. He neither blinks nor
looks at me, stays there, fixed in his shabby robes,
threatening both the cygnet and my praise poem until

I remember the width and grandeur of his wings when he flies
down river and know there can't be a praise poem without him.

One poem, not written for the commission but for my partner's birthday, sneaks into the final pamphlet that we called *Second Wind*. And surprise, surprise, it's a poem about being old and happy!

Watching telly with you

We could go to Paris of course
but not so often. And it might not be quite
as cosy as the sofa, the fire, our slippers,
the zapper. Sometimes mid-morning
I think about it, hankering a little like
the lovelorn do, for that evening lull,
front door locked, feet up, snugged up,
loved up and watching telly with you.

A commission can pull things out of you that you didn't know
were there. A commission's a wonderful thing tra la.

BBC Radio 3, 28 April 2017

A WRITER IN THE BARDO

A book and a birthday have prompted me to look back at my time – twenty years ago – as writer-in-residence, in the palliative care unit of Dumfries & Galloway Royal Infirmary. The book, the winner of the 2017 Man Booker, is *Lincoln in the Bardo* by George Saunders.

The historical seed for this stunningly original novel – which takes place over a single evening in 1862 – is President Lincoln's grief for his son, William 'Willie' Wallace Lincoln, who died of typhus when he was eleven. There were newspaper reports of a grief-stricken Lincoln returning to the crypt several times to hold his boy's body. The Georgetown cemetery where Willie was buried becomes the bardo of Saunders's novel.

The bardo is a Buddhist term for the transitional state between death and re-birth. What happens in this state is defined in *The Tibetan Book of the Dead*. (OUP 1960) In Saunders's novel, the Tibetan Buddhist bardo is merged with a kind of Dantean limbo and Catholic purgatory. Willie is not alone. The cemetery is populated by a horde of spirits unwilling or unable to complete the journey, to truly die. The novel, full of quotes real and fictional, is told in the many voices of these restless souls.

Without being able to go along with the notion of reincarnation, this post-death process – borrowed by Saunders from *The Tibetan Book of the Dead* – from acknowledging one actually *is* dead, through a karmic replay of one's past, plus visits from various deities, contains, for me, a wonderfully logical imagination. One is not just dead-dead. One's spirit is going off somewhere. Taking its time.

The novel took me back to the Alexandra Unit (the palliative care unit) in Dumfries which, in retrospect, seemed a kind of bardo, the patients there being beyond cure, in transition if you like, between life and death. I remembered how some of the patients had strange morphine dreams which seemed to bear some resemblance to karmic replays. Who is to know? Memory and morphine can bring up strange narratives. I remember L, who in his eighties had a powerful memory of his school teacher who had been shell-shocked. L himself had played in a dance band in Glasgow. Sometimes in his confused state he forgot he was in hospital and thinking he was at home demanded that the nurse bring him the memorabilia from his dance band days.

Mostly I wrote the stories, memories and poems those still well enough to tell them, told me. In B's case it was almost an entire potted biography from his childhood in the Gorbals to his time in the navy.

Another patient dictated a letter to his daughters. 'Never say no to a hug,' he told them which made me cry. E wrote a sonnet about the arrival of her baby brother; H, a shepherd, told of his month on the hill at lambing time; A, a farmer's daughter, told of her one sweetheart, a padre in the war who never came back. Sometimes a relative, waiting days and nights at a bedside, found relief in talking.

In the late nineties, this was quite a pioneering residency. Funded by an endowment to the hospital's palliative care unit and partly by what was then the Scottish Arts Council . Within the context of palliative care – emotional support, dignity, help with bereavement – having a writer on board was thought to be therapeutic. I was to work mainly with cancer patients, but also staff and relatives. It never seemed possible to prove the therapeutic value of the residency in some kind of statistical way, though I have absolutely no doubt that it was. Patients in hospital are done-unto. I was there wanting something from them, a story, something that would tell others about their lives after they'd gone. Patients had something to give. After death, their relatives often asked if there was something written, a caught memory, a message, something said, something the next-best-thing to lasting.

Looking back at my time at the hospital, what surprises me now is the sudden ache it gives me – a pang like long delayed grief. I'm surprised because I'd regarded the year as one of the most important of my life. I'd had a strong sense of purpose. I'd made good friends. Publishing a collection of poems and stories by patients had given me a sense of achievement. The post was challenging, yes, sometimes heart-rending, but intensely satisfying and for me – well, happy.

So why the ache? I think it's to do with so much hope. Lately there have been so many stories which could carry the headline of *Fighting to Survive*. It isn't just the agony of parents fighting to keep a very ill child alive, it's somehow everyone, everywhere. These days to fight a terminal prognosis, to try all remedies, to travel to whatever country offers new help, seems almost expected Against all odds, against all ills, against all cancers, patients hope. It's re-activated the memory of hope in the bardo of the Alexandra Unit. It's not the dying of those patients who I listened to and scribed for, that has caused this ache. It's the memory of their hope.

Sue Black, one of the world's leading anatomists and forensic anthropologists writes, in her book *All That Remains: a life in death* (Doubleday, 2018) that 'where in the past we might have accepted a terminal prognosis and turned to a church to ensure the health of our souls, now we are more likely to trawl the internet in search of every last vestige of temporal hope that might keep us alive for just a little bit longer.'

Even Tessa Jowell, who spoke so movingly in the House of Commons urging research into brain cancer, was driven by hope to search for a cure outside the UK, consulting medics in America and seeing a consultant in Germany. Hope fuels energy, though not always.

In *The Guardian* of May 12, 2018 Owen Jones took issue with what he called 'the death taboo – the whole narrative of cancer as a battle … with this implication that you either win or lose on your own steam.' His father, Jones writes, was 'just the bewildered victim of a malign invisible force that beat him up and then killed him. His own attitude had no bearing on his fate.'

In an earlier *Guardian* (19.3.18) the famous potter, Edmund de Waal, reading books submitted for the Wellcome book prize, wrote that 'there is change in the public space around death.' Praising the hospice movement and the training in palliative care as one of 'the most compassionate changes to occur in the last thirty years,' de Waal suggests that this change is slowly moving outside the hospitals, clinics and hospices.

I'm writing this during a week that's been called 'Good Death Week'. Maybe there is just something perverse in my nature that dislikes this soubriquet. You don't have to think for long to realise that there are all too many absolutely dreadful deaths. There's also the current (fashionable?) notion of 'death cleaning' whereby you have a very major clear out, to save your offspring the trouble. Well yes, I can go along with this, though not very cheerily.

Which brings me to thoughts of my next birthday. I've had more than my three score years and ten. Death is on my mind. And I feel bad about the question that keeps lingering in my head when I read another battle to survive story – what about giving up gracefully? Isn't this 'fight' slightly unseemly, like staying too long at the party? Of course I shall probably be just the same – clinging on for, what do they say, *for dear life?* But I hope not.

When, twenty years ago, I applied for the post of writer-in-residence, I gave a lot of thought to my motives. Mostly I felt they were all wrong, at least possibly all wrong by NHS standards – being not entirely unselfish. First of all, it meant working in what seemed to me to be the border land between life and death and I thought that's where a writer ought to be. (I remember seeing my first dead body and being absolutely astonished at how empty of person it was). Also, as death then and now really is mostly kept so hidden, I thought I might actually learn how to die well. I wanted to be useful. Sitting at a desk writing and throwing much of it away even now doesn't feel very useful. Last, but by no means least, I thought the post might be a homeopathic cure for hypochondria. It wasn't!

Now thinking back to my time as writer-in-residence, I

particularly remember S, a young mother whose angry poems included a prayer that she be allowed to live to look after her children. S didn't want the peace and quiet and comfort of the palliative care unit. She wanted the noise, the comings and goings, the *life* of the downstairs wards where hope still existed.

She left letters for her children.

Royal Literary Fund, August 6, 2018 (www.rlf.org.uk)

SLEEP

Last night was a bad one. In bed by eleven, still awake at two. Try reading. Try stomping around. Try *Paracetamol*. Wake Beloved who is snoring sweetly in spare room, for one of those wee-small-hours conversations about the state of the world/my life. Sleep three until six. Hope Radio 4 might give me another hour. It doesn't.

I'm not what you'd call a *serious* insomniac. I average two good nights to one bad night. But 'good' is rarely more than five hours and bad can range from totally sleepless to a restless hour or two. Sometimes getting to the Shipping Forecast at 5.30 a.m. is, ironically, like reaching dry land.

Yes, yes, I know I should do something about it. But somehow I'm protective of my insomnia. It's mine. Almost my doppelganger. It takes the temperature of my psyche. It knows what I'm about. It's quite dramatic. In a curious way, the insomniac state is very particular. There's an aloneness. I have a feeling of being closer to my subconscious than when either properly awake or properly asleep.

Sometimes after a sleepless night I feel quite light-headed, as if I'm living in a state of heightened perception. Sometimes after a sleepless night I just feel groggy.

To have a good night (i.e. five hours) sleep my psyche needs to be in a state of equilibrium. That doesn't happen often enough. As soon as my head hits the pillow I discover I'm anxious or angry, in despair, in panic, or all of a buzz with a jumble of grammarless thoughts.

I have a range of sleep-inducing routines. Reading (preferably a book that's gripping but not over exciting). Breathing exercises. Lying on the floor with my legs up the wall which is sometimes successful though I worry that if Beloved should venture from his nice sleep/snory room into mine, he might think I'm dead. Recitation. I do a lot of this. Alphabetical cities from from

Amsterdam to Zanzibar. Girls' names. Boys' names. I take imaginary journeys – usually to my mother-in-law's flat via May Terrace, a pretty and mysteriously quiet street behind the Giffnock railway station. I have a song or two I sing. I say the Lord's Prayer. I've been saying the Lord's Prayer since I was about seven when I had to say it ten times over without a mistake to make sure the bogey man didn't come. ('What was that mumbo jumbo you were muttering' my mother would ask years later.) Counting backwards from a hundred. A cup of tea. 2mg diazepam (just now and again, honest). Waking up Beloved is a last resort and he's amazingly kind about it.

I used to listen to the World Service. I was particularly fond of a cricket programme called 'Stumps' which was hypnotically boring and sent me off before anything actually happened. Though maybe nothing ever did. But since the pandemic, the World Service has become so full of woe, so full of awful stories, that it's no longer soporific. Late night Radio 4 Extra seems fond of comedies with canned laughter. Radio 3's music just isn't bland and boring enough to send me off.

Of course it isn't only the confusion of the mind that keeps me awake. As I age, physical problems join in. Burning feet, restless legs, night sweats, hypertension, sore back, uncomfortable tum etc etc.

My yoga teacher (whose ghost I wish I could conjure up at night) was brilliant at putting her students into a completely relaxed state. I loved how she ended a class with what I think of as a prayer –

May I be free from suffering.
May I be as happy and healthy as it's possible for me to be.
May I have ease of being.

Awake or asleep, it's *ease of being* I covet.

I recognise in myself that all too common desire not to be

cured of one's faults, ailments, sins. I seem to stick to my insomnia the way some women stick with an abusive husband. At what point might I really do something about it? Stop blathering on about how Maggie Thatcher survived on five hours sleep at night (but look at what happened to her in the end?) and make an effort. What is it in me that somehow doesn't want to be soothed, placated, made somehow virtuous by sleeping for seven hours a night?

I do have an Insomnia Chum. Elizabeth, like me, has good nights and bad nights. It's comforting to think of others being awake. (I'm cheered by a lit window at 3 am). Sometimes I get out of bed, go to my study and send Elizabeth a long email. She appears in a poem I've written called *The Insomniac's Café*. My poem is really a 'take' on one of my favourite Hemingway stories, *A Clean, Well-Lighted Place*. In Hemingway's story there are two waiters, one young, one old, and a deaf old man who sits and drinks brandy and who last week had attempted suicide. The young waiter wants to go home to bed. The older waiter understands the experience of nothingness, that many an insomniac knows, the *nada nada nada* that only a clean, well lit place, can make bearable. Here's my poem.

The Insomniac's Café

A shuttle shaped much like a CT scanner
will deliver you there.
It's open all night of course.
Lighting dim, rugs ready, a booth
to yourself.
Elizabeth will be there already.
You will have your passport –
sleeping pills, package of nightmares,
a recording of those incomprehensible nagging voices.

The soft-footed attendant
who has been there forever will see to you.
His pad   pad   pad
will comfort you like a lullaby.
You can order a dream
though there's no guarantee
it will arrive. It doesn't matter.
It's enough that you're not alone.

I think my 'soft-footed attendant' is probably Hemingway's old waiter still hanging on in there.

But writing this blog has made me remember my very first sleepless night. I was eleven. It was Christmas time and the house being full of family visitors, I was to sleep in the spare room. The spare room spent most of the year shrouded in ghostly dust sheets. It was a room in which a bird had died. It was a room with two doors. Using an imaginary child named Hetty, I wrote about the night in a short story called *The Spare Room*. Here's an extract:

'*When a bird dies in a room,* says Mags, *it means a murderer will come.* Hetty lies in the dead centre of the big bed that grows bigger and bigger and she lies there watching first the left door, then the right door as if held transfixed by some nightmare tennis match. She is waiting for the slow turning of a door knob. She is thinking about the bird and how long it took to die and with what blind panic it would have hurled itself at window, door, ceiling. She is thinking about Aunt Lily's lost soul and Mags's murderer.'

The story ends with the line 'something of the old Hetty stays, like the bird, locked in the spare room'.

Maybe this explains it all. I've been psychologically locked in that spare room all these years. I need to get out. Sleep in the garden. Buy a tent.

Autumn Voices, August 2021 (www.autumnvoices.co.uk)

NOTES ON *LEARNING TO SLEEP* BY JOHN BURNSIDE, CAPE, £10.00

So, o.k. I know this isn't going to be a How To book but I can't help hoping there might be a tip or two from a poet renowned for both his poems and his insomnia. Let me begin.

It's a hard read. I start at the Notes & Acknowledgements (Isn't this where every writer starts?) Next, the endorsements, one of which has Burnside described as a genius. I immediately feel a bit inadequate. Can one criticise a genius? Or if one fails to understand his work is it because one is too stupid? Putting such thoughts aside, I turn to the blurb which tells me that Burnside's insomnia which led to his recent near-death experience will inform the latter part of the book. Serious suspense! Can't wait.

This is Burnside's first collection of poetry in four years. The publishers say this as if he's been hanging about. Actually I gave up trying to keep up with JB some time ago. I like to keep track of a poet who appeals to me but Burnside has become too prolific. I mean fifteen vols so far and that's not counting fiction, non-fiction and autobiography! Life's too short.

On to the poems. There are three sections: Learning to Sleep, Toxic and The Days. Cape's blurb serves as a useful handrail to hang on to. I make a note of 'lost pagan ancestry' and further on, 'a radical pagan sense of celebration'. (Isn't pagan enough without the further qualification of 'radical'?). I note to expect 'a series of provocative meditations on the ways in which we are all harmed by institutions, from organised religion or marriage, to the tawdry concepts of gender and romantic love'. Well, that's a kind of compass guide to the Burnside world.

Jeysus but there are some titles in this collection! *Extinction Sutra/Blind Pig Blues; Aspects of Mental Economy; Preparations for the True Apocalypse; Fake Cochineal.*

The collection contains a number of elegies or ghostly hauntings, including a moving one about Burnside's mother. She appears 'slicing a heart/in my empty kitchen'. (*Indelible*) 'I've never believed in ghosts,' Burnside writes but goes on to recall the 'friend of a friend of a friend/who witnessed a light that nobody could explain'. Somehow this is often where Burnside is – in an inexplicable place yet sensing something there. Sometimes the hauntings seem to be either of his younger or another self (*Toxic* and *Changeling*).

Another elegy is about Rimbaud and is followed by *At Ma Bohème (after Rimbaud).* You feel Rimbaud is a kindred spirit though there is no getting back to the sixteen year old Rimbaud arm in arm with the muse, wandering off with his torn coat pockets and a hole in his breeks. For Burnside 'the Dreamtime is lost' as is The Temple of Baal-Shamin – an ancient Syrian temple dedicated to the sky god. So too is the forest, 'gone to palm-oil/and Merbau decking.'

I had to Google The Temple of Baal-Shamin and Merbau decking. In fact I did a lot of Googling while reading this book. By the end of *At Ma Bohème* Burnside goes on his way 'learning to breathe, like a Seventh Son'. Seventh sons, according to Google, have occult powers.

I got terribly involved researching the background to *Extinction Sutra/ Blind Pig Blues* in which Boethius's *consolatio philosophiae* meets Robert Hicks aka Barbecue Bob (nicknamed after the restaurant where he worked), a Piedmont blues singer. Boethius wrote his consolations while awaiting execution and Barbecue Bob died in 1932 when he was only 29. Both had comparable thoughts on love and time. I liked them unforgettably yoked together in this way. Despite listening to a CD of Barbecue Bob I still felt the need to check out the Buddha's Extinction Sutra. (Back to Google.)

Buddha says to Ananada 'when the Dharma is about to perish, during the evil age of the five turbidities, the way of demons will flourish.' I thought there were no demons in *Learning to Sleep,* but then I found 'old demons/ watching from the murk' (*At Notre Dame de Reims*)

The two poems directly linked to sleep (though there is something dreamlike or hypnagogic about the whole collection) – are the title poem and *Ode to Hypnos*. *Learning to Sleep* reads like a Grimm fairy tale. It opens with a hunter who 'returns/at first light, bearing a heart/in which all warmth has ceased'. By the end of the poem there's reference to Rose Red (sister to Sleeping Beauty?) and the hunter is 'rinsing the glit from his knife'. *Ode to Hypnos* (god of sleep) has 'the angel of slumber, come from the woods/to press a bloody talon to the glass'. Nightmares perhaps? Or was this the near-death experience?

Then there are the 'provocative meditations'. Well, there's a poem about a betrothal in which the couple have a serpentine hosepipe in their Home Counties garden and where 'wedlock falls out of fashion/like bliss, or sin.' In *A Brief Memo, for Valentine's Day*, the narrator appears to cut out what might have been his heart but turns out to be an ivory white bone. Whatever it is, it won't come back to life so he buries it under a thorn. I suspect that's romance done for.

Two of the poems I particularly liked are *Hether Blether* and *At Notre Dame de Riems*. *Hether Blether* is another elegy-come-haunting poem based on the story of a Rousay girl from a hidden island who disappeared. Her vanishing leaves 'silence/hanging in the hallway/like a fog.' *At Notre Dame de Reims* describes the animal sculptures of the cathedral, the mason's art that provides 'a refuge for the pagan' and allows Burnside a happy definition of lust 'in the old tongue' as 'no more/ than pleasure: no-one's/ shame and not a sin.'

There are lines in *Learning to Sleep* that make you catch your breath: This, from *Indelible*, which I take to be about the language shared with his mother.

> 'our pagan dialect
> of locked grimoires
> and back street skipping rhymes'.

And   'like that ache
       behind the lungs
       that never comes to song.' (*Hether Blether*)

But there are a number of poems that despite re-readings, remained closed to me. I was relieved that the final poem, *Poscript,* was a sonnet, and to find Burnside

               on the brink
of elsewhere, gazing out across the land,
as if a better world was still to come.

On the brink of elsewhere. I think this is where Burnside always lives.

Autumn Voices, August 2021 (www.autumnvoices.co.uk)

A DANGEROUS JOB

For more than twenty years I've been reviewing books for *The Spectator*. I can't remember *how* I began, though it's pleasing to note that I've weathered – if that's the right word for a twenty year stint – two literary editors and two poetry editors.

I think I slid into reviewing via poems. Between 1989 and 1995, the poet and novelist P J Kavanagh, then the Poetry Editor, accepted just under a dozen poems, one or two a year. It's probable he rejected twice as many. At any rate in 1996 he retired and I didn't publish another poem in *The Spectator* until 201l.

But in 1985 (approx.) Mark Amory became Literary Editor. Did he inherit me from P J? Or was I brazen and asked if I might review a book? I've no idea, but in March 2001 my first book review was published. It was Hanif Kureishi's *Gabriel's Gift*. Amory attached an appreciative post-it to my contributor's copy.

In retrospect, what's astonishing about my novice status, is that it's taken me forty years to graduate from being a short-hand typist in the Literary Department of *The Sunday Times* – typing up the copy for such eminences as Cyril Connolly – to reviewing fiction for *The Spectator*. It's where life has landed me, rather than this being my intended direction. But I can't help feeling that it's pleasingly neat, completes a circle, in my end is my beginning, so to speak.

And now that I'm an occasional but regular writer in *The Spectator* I can't help but think back to those heady days at *The Sunday Times* when I was young and foolish and all literary London seemed to call into the Literary Department. I look at photos of Sam Leith (current literary editor, of *The Spectator* whom I've never met) and remember the distinguished Jack Lambert in his bow tie and floaty grey hair and the young Michael Ratcliffe fresh from Oxford or Cambridge, cutting and pasting long wet galley proofs of print that made up the book review pages. Most of all I remember the great wall of shelves stacked with books of every kind sent by publishers of every ilk.

But back or onwards (memory works in both directions) to 2001 and Hanif Kureishi. After him came Wendy Cope's *If I Don't Know* which instantly alerted me to the dangers of reviewing books. Cope had responded to a review by Robert O'Brien of her first book, *Making Cocoa for Kingsley Amis,* in which he suggested she 'wrote to amuse'. Cope replied with a sharp rebuke in her next collection, *Serious Concerns:*

> *Write to amuse? What an appalling suggestion*
> *I write to make people anxious and miserable and to worsen*
> *their indigestion.*

And on *Woman's Hour* she'd remarked that some reviews of *If I Don't Know* had been 'a bit iffy'. I vowed never to be 'iffy' and with one exception, I never reviewed poetry again. It's too close to my heart and poets are too stroppy. I stuck to fiction. I think of myself as a good reader rather than a critic, one qualified via an M.Litt and the reading of many novels, to write about them. In addition I spent a number of years writing features for provincial newspapers. I'm trained in two skills. Meeting a deadline and writing to order of a specific number of words.

Although on a map, my writing journey from *The Sunday Times* Literary Department (via various collections of poems, short stories, children's books, writing residencies and the like) to writing for *The Spectator* looks obvious, it still surprises me. Very few of my friends read *The Spectator* and until I began having poems accepted, neither did I. Now, politics aside, I'm a keen reader of the journal and rather proud to be one of its writers.

Some of this has to be to do with tone of voice, with somehow having an appreciation of the readership you are writing for. Without quite knowing how, I think I've picked up that tone of voice in the way you do when finding yourself in a particular community. You probably do it first when at school, developing one way of speaking with friends, another way at home. My

Spectator voice is, somehow, my own. I'm at ease in it.

During Mark Amory's reign I was allowed more space than I am now. Looking back I see I was given eight hundred words for Saul Bellow's *Collected Stories* and almost a thousand for Amos Oz's *A Tale of Love and Darkness*. One year I was invited to the famous *Spectator* summer party, regarded as 'the place to be seen'. Possibly it was when Boris Johnson was editor in chief. Held in the garden at the back of *The Spectator* office, then in Doughty Street, there was a lot of alcohol and a lot of people I neither knew nor recognised. Maybe I didn't drink enough or talk enough, but I've never been invited again. I suspect the invitation was a mistake.

When in 2014 (24 reviews down) Mark Amory retired, I thought my time might be up. But lo, the amenable Sam Leith took over and Hugo Williams became Poetry Editor. I was twice lucky. But Sam, eminently approachable, a man prompt in replying to any email even on a Sunday night, is a slightly harder task-master than Amory, rarely asking for a review longer than 500 words.

I read a great many other reviews. *The London Review of Books* reviews are really major essays, often printing them weeks if not months after the book's publication date. They can be informative, thought provoking, elegant and having read one, you don't always need to read the book. I personally dislike the kind of review that tells you the story or content of the book at length but never ventures an opinion. An opinion is what I'm looking for. An opinion is what I try to conclude with in my own reviews.

If I'd ever thought that being paid to read books was a job made in heaven, the notion was squashed early on with the discovery of the work involved. The hard work lies mainly in condensing what you want to say into very few words. Cutting a review down to the four or five hundred words asked for can require a number of drafts. Blaise Pascal identified the problem when, apologising for a long letter, he remarked that if he'd had more time he would have written a shorter one.

I often find it necessary to read not only the book for review, but the author's previous works or at least some of them. When Ann Patchett's second collection of essays, *These Precious Days,* arrived on my doorstep, she was new to me. I felt I had to read her first collection *This is the Story of a Happy Marriage*, plus a couple of her novels, *The Dutch House* and *Truth and Beauty.* All of which, even though I'm a quick reader, takes time both for reading and for making notes. And extra time for pondering. I suspect pondering is the most important part. It means the thoughts gathering and shaping in the mind; a few sentences making themselves known. Pondering allows me to work out what I want to say.

Reviewing Emma Donaghue's 2022 novel, *Haven,* it was only through reading her earlier novels that I could recognise her constant theme of confinement – *Room* sparked by the story of Joseph Fritzel, who held his daughter captive; *The Pull of the Stars,* set in a small maternity ward; *The Wonder* set in a cabin and *Haven* set on a former monastic site on a remote island. Wide reading also made me aware of the Catholic element in Donaghue's work. It's reading in depth really and there's both satisfaction and pleasure in this, though as a way to earn a living, it's silly. We've moved on from the days when journalists were paid by the line. Even so, unless you're a big name, the renumeration is fairly minimal.

It's possible, of course, to over-read. Looking at *The Spectator* for March 2020, I see I began by saying I thought it was perhaps a mistake to read Sebastian Barry's *Days Without End* before reading its sequel, *A Thousand Moons,* for the two had begun to merge in my head. Over-reading was also a problem with Jennifer Egan's *Candy House*. 'It's hard to decide', I wrote 'if it's an advantage to have read the Pulitzer prize winning *Goon Squad* first or if it just makes reading *Candy House* more like the sort of memory test that could mess with your head.' My verdict? 'A dizzying and disturbing mishmash of family saga, sci-fi and literary high jinks.'

Apart from reading other work by the writer being reviewed, it is all too tempting to Google other reviews – though as you risk being influenced, it's best not to do so until you've written your own.

I try to write fair, honest criticism. I try to keep in mind that writing a novel is a considerable achievement. I aim to give the gist of the story, say something about the author, more about the actual writing, and a final opinion. I'm mostly appreciative. I rarely reach to the acerbic in a review. 'Nothing explored in any depth' is as dismissive as I get. Or, on Roddy Doyle's twelfth novel *Love* – 'is not Doyle's trade-mark conversation between two men in a pub a little interminable?' Just a bit spikey.

One of the pitfalls of reviewing books is becoming aware of your own prejudices. When I was sent Benjamin Myers's historical novel *Cuddy*, I began by reading his previous book *The Gallows Pole* which had far too much violence in it for my taste. I had to hide the cover I hated it so much. I didn't much care for the material on Myers's website either, or, if I'm honest, the look of the man, so there was quite a lot to overcome before I found *Cuddy* (the story of St Cuthbert) to be as full of grace and vision as *The Gallows Pole* had been of violence and was then able to admire its 'dazzling compendium of styles: poetry, prose, dramatic dialogue' as well as its research and its lyrical depiction of Cumbrian landscape.

Occasionally, if I'm quick off the mark in learning of a book about to be published by a writer I really, really like, I'm able to ask for it to review. In twenty years there have been three: Amos Oz, W.S. Graham, Claire Keegan.

I've read almost everything Amos Oz has written so in my one escape from fiction, I was delighted to be able to review his 2004 memoir, *A Tale of Love and Darkness*. Writing this now, in 2023, during the traumatic war between Israel and Gaza, it's salutary to look back at what I wrote then: 'The personal element in Oz's tale, the time it has taken to find peace with himself, can only make us think – as he surely intends us to do – about the time it might take for the two peoples of Israel and Palestine also to find peace.'

Oz was a strong peace activist.

Jonathan Freedland in *The Guardian* of October 2023 wrote that 'Oz was never wiser than when he described the Israel-Palestine conflict as something infinitely more tragic' (than a clash between right versus wrong) but 'a clash of right versus right. Two peoples' with deep wounds, howling with grief, fated to share the same small piece of land.'

2004 must have been a good year for me because I also reviewed W.S. Graham's *New & Collected Poems*. Graham is a poet I've loved for many years so I was very pleased to be given his *New & Collected Poems*. My review describes his poems as the most talkative poems of the 20th century. 'They talk to the reader, to friends (dead and alive), to his wife, to himself (or selves), to the muse, to silence, to the alphabet and, perhaps most importantly, to language itself.'

I find it strange that *The Spectator* publishes new poems but rarely reviews poetry. Perhaps it's too risky. Perhaps it says something about its readership.

More recently, I've become a fan of the Irish writer, Claire Keegan. Her output isn't vast and I've read everything she has written so far. Keegan has a Fiction Clinic and gives many talks and workshops in Ireland, England and Australia. In early September 2023 I received an email telling me that she would be delivering three seminars in Wexford on 'How Fiction Works' while down the road at Kilmore Quay's Write by the Sea Festival, *Faber* would be launching her new hardback, *So Late in the Day*. I was excited! I emailed Sam Leith. I wondered, if perhaps *The Spectator* might send me to Kilmore Quay, but alas, Sam said he had no money for jollies. However, I could review the book. I was delighted. I also felt quite proud of myself for having brought *So Late in the Day* to his attention and consoled myself that instead of the slog of travelling and going to a festival, I could do what I like doing best of all – sit at home and read a book.

AUTHOR'S NOTE

Only when I'd put these essays together did I realise that they encompass my writing life from my early twenties as a gauche Young Thing in the Literary Department of *The Sunday Times* to my slightly cranky eighties reviewing fiction for *The Spectator*.

Inbetween I've worked as a journalist, an English teacher in a secondary school, a tutor in Eng. Lit. at a university, a tutor on various creative writing courses, a writer-in-residence at a hospital, a Royal Literary Fund Fellow, a children's author visiting schools; a poet giving readings and workshops.

In retrospect, these all feel like parts I've played, hats I've worn, while the *real life*, the life that involves putting words on paper, has carried on like a bass continuo or a heartbeat. Sometimes I think that it's all been about listening in, trying to catch a poem or story that starts off by me but, just sometimes, achieves a life of its own.

ACKNOWLEDGEMENTS

I've been accompanied on the 'journey' covered in these essays by many companions, a few no longer with us. So this is rather like a lifetime's thank you letter.

At *The Sunday Times,* J.W. Lambert, Michael Ratcliffe and John Gay Davis sent me on my way into journalism. I became a children's writer under the editorship of Julia MacRae, the wonderful Delia Huddy (first of Walker Books and then Random House) and Wendy Boase of Walker Books plus the help and encouragement of agents Lindsey Fraser and Kathryn Ross. For support, friendship and wisdom during a year's writing residency at Dumfries & Gallowy Royal Infirmary I'd like to thank Dr Lindsay Martin, David Foreman, Liz Rae, Olivia Richardson and the artist, Rachel Mimiec. These essays are littered with poems most of which might not have seen the light of day without Harry Chambers of Peterloo Poets, Hamish Whyte of Mariscat Press and Peter Carpenter of Worple Press. My thanks also to Gerry Cambridge of *The Dark Horse* who commissioned and published at least two of these essays and to the science writer, Philip Ball, without whom I'd never have appeared in the pages of *Chemistry World.* At *The Spectator,* P.J. Kavanagh, Mark Amory, Hugo Williams and Sam Leith have kept me in print. Thank you. My love and thanks to my very dear writing chums/helpmates: Kate Hendry, Anne and Henry Kernighan, U.A. Fanthorpe, Dr R.V. Bailey, Vivian French, Robyn Marsack, Tom Pow, Stewart Conn, Elizabeth Cook, Lesley Glaister, Sarah LeFanu, Christine De Luca, Ian McDonough and most of all my partner, publisher and poet Hamish Whyte.